The Shaws of Terenure

Maynooth Studies in Local History

SERIES EDITOR Raymond Gillespie

This volume is one of six short books published in the Maynooth Studies in Local History series in 2010. Like over 85 of their predecessors they range widely over the local experience in the Irish past. That local experience is presented in the complex social world of which it is part, from the world of the dispossessed Irish in 17th-century Donegal to political events in 1830s Carlow; from the luxury of the early 19th-century Dublin middle class to the poverty of the Famine in Tipperary; and from the political activists in Kimmage in 1916 to those who suffered in a different sort of war as their homes were bombed in South Circular Road in 1941. These local experiences cannot be a simple chronicling of events relating to an area within adminis-trative or geographically determined boundaries since understanding the local world presents much more complex challenges for the historian. It is a reconstruction of the socially diverse worlds of poor and rich as well as those who took very different positions on the political issues that preoccupied the local societies of Ireland. Reconstructing such diverse local worlds relies on understanding of what the people of the different communities that made up the localities of Ireland had in common and what drove them apart. Understanding the assumptions, often unspoken, around which these local societies operated is the key to recreating the world of the Irish past and reconstructing the way in which those who inhabited those worlds lived their daily lives. As such, studies such as those presented in these short books, together with their predecessors, are at the forefront of Irish historical research and represent some of the most innovative and exciting work being undertaken in Irish history today. They also provide models which others can follow up and adapt in their own studies of the Irish past. In such ways will we understand better the regional diversity of Ireland and the social and cultural basis for that diversity. If they also convey something of the vibrancy and excitement of the world of Irish local history today they will have achieved at least some of their purpose.

Maynooth Studies in Local History: Number 91

The Shaws of Terenure
A nineteenth-century Dublin merchant family

Tony Mc Carthy

FOUR COURTS PRESS

Set in 10pt on 12pt Bembo by
Carrigboy Typesetting Services for
FOUR COURTS PRESS LTD
7 Malpas Street, Dublin 8, Ireland
www.fourcourtspress.ie
and in North America for
FOUR COURTS PRESS
c/o ISBS, 920 N.E. 58th Avenue, Suite 300, Portland, OR 97213.

ISBN 978–1–84682–262–9

Printed in Scotland by
Thomson Litho, Glasgow.

Contents

Acknowledgments

Many people have helped and contributed, in varying ways, in researching and writing this short book. To the staffs of the following libraries and archives I offer thanks for their courteous and professional assistance: the Russell and John Paul libraries in NUI Maynooth, National Library of Ireland, National Archives of Ireland, the British Library, Dublin City Library, Pearse Street, Dublin City Archives, Trinity College Registrar's Office, the Masonic Lodge of Ireland Library and the Fingal County Council Archives.

My thanks to Professor Raymond Gillespie, for his guidance, willingness to share his immense intellect and above all for his enthusiasm for his subject. A special word of thanks must go to my thesis supervisor Professor Colm Lennon. Colm is a gentleman with whom it was a pleasure to work. He provided direction and guidance and gave great encouragement. The study was significantly enhanced by his input. I greatly appreciated his wise council.

To Dr Terry Dooley and Mr Rob Goodbody of NUI Maynooth for the insights provided to the science of local history. To Gary Gartland for his help in the presentation of the thesis upon which this work is based. To Cathy Scufil for allowing me access to her research material relating to the family.

I would also like to pay tribute to Tom Kelly a graduate of the MA in local history class of 2009. Those of us who were lucky enough to know Tom will acknowledge the contribution he made to our enjoyment of the program. Unfortunately Tom died prematurely earlier this year. I would like to express my condolences to his family and to acknowledge his contribution.

To my children Colm, Liam and Sinead.

Last, but not least, to my wife Anita, who as usual put up with my quirks and obsessions and still remains with me. At this stage I think she's sorry she ever heard of the Shaws of Terenure.

Introduction

While much has been written about the great landowning families of Ireland, little, with the odd exception, has been written about the prominent middle-class merchant families who dominated Dublin and Irish life in the late 18th and 19th centuries. Unlike the more industrialized countries such as Britain and the United States, where families such as the Rothschilds, Morgans, Vanderbilts or Bearings have become part of the historical landscapes, their Irish equivalents have for the most part been reduced to historical footnotes. Although some might suggest that this situation exists because their historical significance is minimal, this author would argue that this is not the case, and that direct legacies of many of these families live on to this day as an integral part of the fabric of Irish economy, for example AIB Group (Shaw), Bank of Ireland (La Touche), Diageo (Guinness), Irish Distillers (Jameson), A&L Goodbody Solicitors (Goodbody). This study is a small attempt to address this deficit by part exploring the history of one such family, namely, the Shaws of Terenure.

At its simplest it is the story of the family during the years 1786 to 1876 told by looking at the lives of four of its patriarchs, Robert Shaw senior (1749–96), his son Robert, first baronet (1774–1849) and his sons Robert, second baronet (1796–1869) and Frederick, third baronet (1799–187 it is not a full family history in the sense of looking at the broader family or their personal triumphs or tragedies over the period but rather it seeks to explore the family's business, social and political lives and in so doing provide some insight into their world and the communities they interacted with. It is the story of how, through the energies of the first two Roberts, the family rose to become leading figures in the commercial life of Dublin in the late 18th century, and how this success enabled the family to establish a platform to enter politics and become central characters in the social scene of Dublin. While of necessity many of the family's achievements are highlighted the emphasis in this study is on the everyday aspects of their lives with the object of trying to explain the context of the social and cultural world in which they operated.

On a wider level, the story is that of a wealthy middle-class family, at a time when there was a major shift in the balance of power and influence from the landed aristocracy to the merchants, industrialists and bankers, who would become the real power brokers in political and commercial life in the 19th century and beyond. This class, for the most part, embraced the free market ideals expounded in the writings of Adam Smith, Ricardo and Malthus. These early exponents of the then-emerging theories of political economy argued that markets needed to regulate themselves through the forces of supply and demand, and that regardless of the consequences, governments should not intervene. By contrast to this *laissez faire* approach in economics, however, the prevailing religious and moral code of the period made social indifference all but impossible and placed a responsibility on the middle classes for those less fortunate than themselves. This paternalistic approach to society was evident in the lives of the four central figures of this story and the study will provide many examples of its practical application. The study will also provide many examples of the preoccupation of the middle classes with causes of various hues, particularly those with a moral or religious overtone. The much-talked of Protestant work ethic that many believe was the cornerstone of the industrial revolution and the basis for many of the world's leading economic powers is also evident in the lives of the characters in this history, as indeed is the preoccupation with class in terms of a focus on ancestry and education.

The history of this particular strand of the family can be traced back to the battle of the Boyne in 1690. William Shaw who was born in Hampshire of Scottish descent *c.*1651, came to Ireland as a soldier in the army of William III.[1] He was made a captain and fought at the Battle of the Boyne in General Ponsonby's army. As a result he was awarded lands at Sandpitts, near Thomastown, Co. Kilkenny, and in Ballinderry, Co. Tipperary. Little is known of the family's early life in Ireland save that William had three sons and a daughter. One of these sons, Robert, married a Mary Markham of Fanningstown, Co. Kilkenny in 1736 and the couple had four children, the youngest of whom was the first Robert of this story. The family was obviously reasonably well connected because they were able, through the good offices of the earl of Bessborough, to secure a position in Dublin for the 15-year-old Robert in the Irish Post Office.[2]

The emergence of the movement for Catholic emancipation and the consequent erosion of Protestant dominance on civic and national politics form a backdrop to the family's involvement in business, politics and the Dublin social scene. Through the words of the family, the reader can hopefully get a glimpse of how the major historical events of the day such as the act of Union, the subsequent Repeal movement, Catholic emancipation, and the Famine were viewed by a wealthy Protestant family.

Despite their prominence, there has been very little written and nothing published about the Shaw family of Terenure. Apart from passing references in a number of books dealing with the politics of 19th-century Ireland, biographies of the family's relative, George Bernard Shaw, a brief family history in *Burke's peerage*, some personal profiles of family members in biographical dictionaries and more comprehensive references to Robert Shaw, first baronet, in Milne's *History of the Royal Bank of Ireland*, the family have all but disappeared from Irish historical annals.[3] This work is then the first attempt to document the family's history.

The work has been greatly facilitated by the availability of a significant collection of family papers. These include family and business account books, property deeds, last wills and testaments for two of the family's patriarchs, letter books and in the case of Robert Shaw, second baronet, a personal diary covering some periods for the years 1824–6. These family papers are held in a range of repositories including the National Library of Ireland, the National Archives of Ireland, Dublin City Archives and the British Library. In terms of those family members who participated in local and national politics, the author has made use of the Hansard reports of debates in the Westminster parliament, the minute books of the county Dublin Grand Jury in the archives of the Fingal County Council, the *Calendar of ancient records of Dublin* the originals of which are preserved in the Dublin City Library and Archive, and the papers of Sir Robert Peel in the British Library which contain correspondence between Peel and Frederick Shaw. In addition, contemporary newspapers contain a significant number of reports covering the family's social and political activities.

For this study it was felt that a thematic approach would allow for the best use of the material available, specifically the family's pre-eminence in business and politics, but also their wealth management and the lifestyle and social position that emerged from it. The study is structured around these three themes. The first chapter explores the family's involvement in the flour merchant and banking businesses. The second looks at the contrasting lifestyles of the four patriarchal figures but more significantly it looks at how the family created and managed the wealth that funded these lifestyles. The third chapter focuses on those members of the family that were involved in representative politics and explores their attitudes to the major political events of the period. Linking the various themes are the social, business and political networks that the family developed and the communities in which they lived and served. Common also are the personalities and characters that impacted on and influenced the everyday lives of people in the Dublin of the late 18th and 19th centuries.

The origins of this study lie in the author's curiosity about who this family were, and, given their once early prominence, why they should have all but disappeared from the history and folklore of Terenure, despite the continuing prominence there of Bushy Park. If one asks any of the thousands of visitors to the now municipal park who the Shaws were, there will be few if any who have even heard of them. While a street in central Dublin still bears their name, the only remote connections in the locality lie in the Irish name of one of the areas roads, Whitehall Road, which in Irish is called Bothar an Racardair (the Recorder's Road), which is so named because Sir Frederick Shaw, the recorder for Dublin, lived in nearby Kimmage Manor and this along with a public house in Crumlin village called 'The Shaw Arms' are the families only attributable legacies.

1. Merchants and bankers, 1786–1836

The story of the family's rise to prominence started quietly in 1764 when the 15-year-old Robert Shaw arrived in Dublin to take up a junior position in the Irish postal service. The post was obtained through the family's connections with the second earl of Bessborough, Frederick Ponsonby, whose father had been Shaws' grandfather's commander at the Battle of the Boyne. Shaw was clearly an excellent employee as we know that he rose through the ranks to become accountant general, before striking out on his own and establishing what his obituary described as 'the first commercial house in this kingdom, and acquired a large fortune, which few of the nobility could equal'.[1]

Dublin in the second half of the 18th century was undergoing rapid population growth and a boom in consumption fuelled by a long period of peace in Ireland and good markets for agricultural output. The latter was due to the opening up of the American market, the ever-expanding empire and the need to supply troops with food in various European campaigns. The main beneficiaries of this boom, were the large landowners, who saw rents triple in value between 1720 and 1770.[2] The new-found wealth gave rise to a building boom as landlords vied with each other to build the great houses that epitomized the period and defined the Anglo-Irish ascendancy class for generations. Nor was the expenditure on lifestyle confined to rural parts, for, in the period, no self-respecting estate landlord could be without a town house in the country's capital, as they flocked to the newly emerging Georgian squares such as Rutland, Fitzwilliam, Merrion, and Mountjoy. Keen to show that Dublin was not a provincial backwater, the state and civic authorities put in place a major public building programme, which saw such iconic buildings as the parliament house in College Green, the Four Courts, the Customs House and the Rotunda being erected alongside private residences such as Leinster House and Marlborough House. As a 'triumph of elegance' it was a city that its 150,000 citizens could be proud of, and which could rightly claim to be the second city of the empire.[3] Thomas Pakenham described its citizens thus: 'They had a style and a sense of pride, a pride of community, colonial nationalism of a sort, bigoted and narrow as it was, that set them apart from a mere English garrison taking its orders from London.'[4]

Rapid economic growth and the building boom that followed, like that which occurred in our own time, led to a bubble. In a similar manner, there was a massive expansion in the country's money supply with a near quadrupling between the years 1720 and 1770, and a further trebling in the

1 Robert Shaw, the elder

period to 1797.[5] As is often the case, the seeds of economic destruction were taking root and would in the new century give rise to serious problems, particularly in banking circles.

While wealth was still very much measured in terms of one's landholdings, the 18th century saw the emergence of a merchant and industrial class. Historians may argue about Ireland's level of participation in the industrial revolution but there is little doubt that, regardless of the degree of systematic industrialism, the infrastructure necessary to foster industrial development such as efficient transport networks, regulatory and legal institutions and banking facilities were beginning to emerge. The emergence of a new category of Irish mercantile entrepreneur, who saw wealth creation as being a product of hard work, initiative, identification of opportunities and developing a network of political and business contacts helped to shift Irish economic hegemony from the landed classes. Robert Shaw was one of these individuals who would facilitate and epitomize this change.

The first reference to Robert Shaw appears in *Wilson's directory* of 1786 where he is described as a 'Wholesale merchant free of 6% and 10% in the

Custom House, Dublin' and residing at 78 Fleet Street.[6] Fleet Street at the
time was a very fashionable part of town given its proximity to the parliament
house on College Green. An indication of the quality of the street may be had
from Gilbert's description of one of its houses as 'a house and office of a
nobleman'.[7] We also know from the family accounts book for the period that
the house had ten hearths and piped water.[8] While it is unclear when Robert
left the employment of the Postal Service, it is unlikely to have been in 1786
when he is first noted in *Wilson's directory* as in 1783 he is listed as one of the
288 initial investors in the Bank of Ireland subscribing £5,000.[9] A cursory
review of the subscribers highlights the circle within which he operated:

Subscriber	Description	Amount subscribed
David, John and Peter La Touche	Leading private bankers and landowners	£10,000 each
Luke Gardiner	Dublin developer	£10,000
Luke White	Lottery agent	£2,000
Cornelius O'Callaghan	Lord Lismore	£6,800
James Hewitt	Lord Lifford Lord high chancellor	£6,000
Charles Agar	archbishop of Cashel	£4,000
Rt. Hon. William Conyngham	Owner of Slane Castle, founder of the Grand Canal Company and of the Kildare Street Club	£5,000
Sir Nicholas Lawless	Leading private banker	£10,000
Valentine Brown	Limerick Brewer and one of the few Catholic subscribers	£10,000
Rt. Hon. Theo Clements	Brother of the earl of Leitrim	£10,000
Theobold Wolfe	Coach maker; father of Wolfe Tone	£10,000
Abraham Wilkinson	Silk merchant and property owner. Future father in law of Robert Shaw, first baronet	£5,200
Dr Robert Emmet	Father of the Robert Emmet	£2,000

That Robert Shaw should have set himself up in business in the first place
was probably due to the practice of primogeniture, whereby the family fortunes
were vested in the eldest son. Robert was the third son of William Shaw of

Thomastown, Co. Kilkenny and the option of remaining on the family estate seat was unlikely to have been attractive for an ambitious and industrious young man. Unlike traditional landed gentry families of the day, a career in the army would not have been inevitable among the Shaws for a third son like Robert. Industry and business acumen appear to have run in the Shaw family as from relatively small beginnings they had shown that through hard work it was possible to build up considerable wealth through land and estate acquisition and this was obviously not lost on the young Robert.[10]

The account and letter books of the business for the period 1785–90 indicate that it was a highly professional and well-run flour merchant and bill holding business.[11] While trading profit and loss accounts are not available for the relevant years, the entries point to a significant business. For instance, an entry dated 13 December 1790 on the account of a George and Thomas Keogh refers to the 'sale of 7,587 barrels of wheat £11,474 15s. 9d.' The books of account make reference to numerous transactions involving English customers indicating a significant cross-channel business. Entries also point to the firm doing business further a field as in the case of an entry dated 26 December 1785 referring to 'postage of a letter to Cadiz 2s.' and a later entry relating to the sale of rape seed to a client in Rotterdam. While the bulk of the entries relate to transactions involving flour millers and bakers there are other entries that show that the firm's activities extend beyond these areas for example, a March 1791 entry records 'By invoice of 10 hogsheads of claret for the Lovely Peggy, Capt. Mathewson £4,389 13s.' The account books also provide illustrations of significant movement in the price of flour depending on the quality of a particular harvest. For instance, in May 1786 flour was selling at 19s. a bag whereas one year later it has risen by over 30 per cent due to a poorer harvest and was selling at £1 4s. 9d. a bag. One can only imagine the effect such price movements must have had on the incomes of farmers.[12]

A letter dated 14 November 1793 from Robert Shaw to Messrs Wades and Williams indicates his dexterity in explaining fluctuating prices that did not meet with the pleasure of his clients:

Gentlemen,
We have both your favour of the 14th instant with regard to the sale of your flour you may be assured there is no opportunity lost on our part, but your own good sense will point out to you on reflection that nothing would be an inducement in a falling market for bakers to buy more than their immediate consumption if the quantity that arrives in town exceeds the consumption, give the goods at what price you would a certain quantity would remain unsold; that is a general cause as to the first flour. It is not of a quality for fine white bread and too fine for household, so that the bakers will not give the price for the latter and

will not answer for the former. Firsts are never a quick sale unless of the very best quality or that there is a great demand. Seconds or household is what is always the great consumption. We think flour will keep up nearly to its present price and may depend every exertion shall be made on our part. RS & Son.[13]

This letter indicates that the writer not only has a clear understanding of the marketplace but also a good grasp of customer relations. It is remarkably attuned to customer service techniques and the fundamentals of marketing, terms hardly recognizable to 18th-century business people, but nonetheless ever-present pillars of business.

Judging by the names recorded in the account books, the firm of Robert Shaw & Son, as it was called post 1790, dealt in an almost exclusively Protestant world, reflecting no doubt the reality of the times. Names such as Clutterbuck, Taylor, Keys, Holmes, Sparrow, Ashworth, Prim, Fortesque, Bellen, Belton, Roberts, Fleetwood, Max, Readshawe, Strang and Furney far out number likely Catholic names such as Daly, Ward and Roche. The account books also indicate that Shaw maintained a strong client base in and around the family's homeland of Thomastown, Co. Kilkenny. For instance, one of his largest customers is the Bennetsbridge Flour Mill, Bennettsbridge being the neighbouring town to Thomastown. There is also ample evidence of dealings with other members of the Shaw clan, such as William, Thomas, Charles and George. This later point illustrates the family's deep roots in the agricultural sector. Business seems to have been handled on an introductory basis where reputation would have been all important. We see this in the following letter to a Mr David Roche dated 12 November 1793.

Dear Sir,

We have your favour of the 9th instant with an introductory letter from our mutual friend, Mr Lyons. We of course cheerfully accept your commission and hope to execute your business to your satisfaction. With respect to the Bounty Paper in dispute we will either act as referee / Robert Shaw & Son / or will enquire into the particulars and report back to you our opinion as you think proper. The Commissioners of the Revenue are certainly very precise in having all the forms complied with. I do suppose it was either want of attention or error in the dates of the papers that may have occasioned the loss, in general however the Board are indulgent where they see a fair claim that is not strictly conformable to laws. The state of the market and middle price shall be duly forwarded. Middle price this week 31s. 9d. for wheat alone, 28s. 10d. for flour, good seed 16s. to 17s., oats 8s. to 13s. MP 11s.

I am yours RS & Son.[14]

As the above letter makes clear, being a successful merchant did not just entail being able to buy and sell but also to have contacts who could smooth over problems with such bodies as the Revenue Commissioners. This might account for a recurring annual entry in the firm's accounts 'Paid to Mr Smith, Corn Office (Custom House), his Christmas gratuity £2 5s. 6d.'[15] A high level of customer service is also evident in the letters sent to customers, one such sent to Mr Timothy Mara, dated 12 November 1793 indicating that they were prepared to look after their clients' personal needs just as much as their business ones:

> Dear Sir,
> We are only favoured with yours of the 10th current. Agreeable to your desire we have ordered the *Dublin Evening Standard* to be forwarded to you and debit 18s. for the half yearly cost in advance agreeable to the enclosed receipt.
> RS & Son.[16]

The firm's records also illustrate involvement in another phenomenon of the late 18th century, namely the State lottery. The lottery was organized by a State Lottery company and the proceeds were used by government to cover public expenditure projects. Rowena Dudley makes it clear in her book on the subject that, in the late 18th century the Irish State lottery enjoyed significant participation with upwards of 40,000 tickets being sold for each draw.[17] By the standard of the times the prizes were enormous, for example £10,000, and the demand for tickets great. The tickets were distributed throughout Ireland and indeed Britain by authorized 'lottery agents'. These agents obtained the right to sell tickets by first taking out a licence at a cost of £100 per annum and then engaging in an auction organized by the State Lottery Office. The auction worked on the basis of an agent putting in a bid for a minimum number of tickets at a price. At the end of the auction process contracts were awarded by the Lottery Office to the successful bidders, who then sold on the tickets to the public at higher prices. For successful bidders this could be a risky business, as the ultimate price to be paid by the public would depend on the level of interest. However, the risks do not appear to have deterred would-be agents who bid aggressively for the right to sell the tickets. Significant profits could be earned by lottery agents. For instance in 1795 agents paid the Lottery Office £6 12s. 6d. per ticket and sold them on to the public for £7 12s. a margin of over 14 per cent.[18]

Such were the profits that could be earned that the Bank of Ireland made a bid to distribute all lottery tickets. A contemporary of Robert Shaw senior, Luke White of Rathfarnham, was said to have amassed a personal fortune of £500,000 from selling lottery tickets when in 1799 he paid £96,000 for Lord Carhampton's house and estate at Lutterellstown, near Lucan in Co. Dublin.[19]

While Shaw senior was a regular bidder for lottery agencies he does not appear to have been of the more aggressive variety as evidenced by the following quote made by Shaw to a Dublin newspaper in relation to his bid 'As for the lottery from what I can learn of other bidders I do not suppose I have any chance of succeeding'.[20] Despite this, the firm's account books are littered with references to the purchase of tickets on behalf of their customers and with lodging prize money proceeds to their accounts, as the following entry in the account of Mr William Fleetwood demonstrates, '4 October 1786 – purchase of 5 lottery tickets – £40 2s. 6d.'[21]

Given the family's subsequent involvement in banking, what is particularly noticeable about the accounts, especially in the later years, was the high level of bill discounting in which the firm became involved. Bill discounting is the process whereby a person who is in receipt of a bill of exchange, usually obtained for the supply of goods, has the bill encashed or held to his account on deposit with a bank or some other acceptable depository. In the days before specialized retail banking, people and business made use of a variety of establishments such as goldsmiths and well-established merchants to provide safe keeping and bill encashment facilities. The fact that Robert Shaw & Son was engaged in such activity is a reflection on the firm's financial standing in terms of having the reserves to encash the level of bills and its reputation whereby clients were prepared to trust them sufficiently to hold funds on their behalf.

Of course the discounting of bills was not without its dangers, as several letters from the firm to recalcitrant clients illustrate, including this one of 26 January 1796 to a Mr Henry Watson:

> Dear Sir,
> I really never found myself more at a loss than how to proceed on the subject of your debt, considering the whole tenor of your conduct and my own unwillingness to go to extremities. I am very divided. You begin your letter by saying you really want to pay before it is your convenience. However when we look at the facts your only proposal is to pay £300 a year unless the convenience of never paying and I don't know what convenience more there would be … If you had the least regard to your character as a man of business you would have pledged your last shilling rather than suffer a person who had the confidence to advance under the faith of your name to be left for years to battle out a debt so incurred … Upon the whole if so moderate a proposal as taking the bond of the parties that I have already bound and accepting the payment of £300 a year be not complied with I shall not interfere further in my attorney taking the steps he thinks essential and shall merely wait your answer for that purpose.
> I am RS.[22]

The above letter illustrates a number of important aspects as to how business was conducted in the late 18th century. Firstly, honour and reputation were critical and hence Shaw's willingness to question the man's bona fides in this regard. Secondly, it would have been very easy for Shaw to have the debtor thrown into the Dublin Marshalsea prison for non-payment of the debt. The consequence of this latter action would have meant in all likelihood that he would never have received any payment, whereas as subsequent entries in the accounts show, the firm received at least two installments of £300. Indeed the dreaded Marshalsea seems to have been an ever-present threat to debtors in the 18th and 19th centuries in Dublin, as the following petition that appeared in the *Freeman's Journal* of 3 February 1803 shows:

> A citizen of Dublin, who for many years lived in the enjoyment of affluence and comfort, and who after suffering imprisonment for debt of near four years' duration, occasioned by a failure in a mercantile pursuit, has been recently liberated, with a constitution considerably impaired by the hardships of confinement and a total loss of property; and is now left with a wife and family of young children, entirely divested of the means of support, and reduced to the painful and humiliating necessity of appealing to the liberality of his fellow citizens, to enable him resume some species of business for the support of his helpless and distressed family. Subscriptions for the foregoing benevolent purpose will be thankfully received at the banks of the Right Honourable David La Touche & Co. and Messers Robert Shaw & Co.[23]

Unlike many of their business equivalents then and now, the Shaws appear to have drawn a very strict distinction between their personal and commercial lives. This is evident from the fact that as well as the business account books, there also exist family account books in which are recorded numerous entries relating to the granting of mortgages to various people and the purchase of annuities and pensions from individuals. These entries will be covered in greater detail in the next chapter of this work.

A puzzling aspect of both the firm and the family account books is the absence of any reference to borrowings on their behalf. This can only be explained either by the disappearance of bank books from the family papers in the various repositories, or by the firm or the family having sufficient resources in terms of profit and working capital reserves to enable the advances be given without recourse to external borrowings. It would take a more forensic accounting review than is feasible in this study to deal satisfactorily with this issue, so for the moment it remains a mystery.

Given the discounting of bills by the firm and the family, the granting of mortgages, the purchase of annuities and the advancement of loans it is not too surprising to find that before long they involved themselves in banking.

2 Robert Shaw, first baronet

Interestingly, however, this takes place after the death of Robert Shaw senior in July 1796. In keeping with the practice of primogeniture, Robert, was succeeded by his eldest son also Robert, who, keen to ensure continuity, wrote to all customers of the firm on 5 July 1796:

> Gentlemen,
> The purpose of the present is to inform you that our very worthy partner Robert Shaw senior died at Cork, Saturday last, and that the business will be continued as usual and you may rest assured that what ever you are pleased to transact with our house shall be attended to with the same care and punctuality which you have always experienced.
> I am RS.[24]

As the subsequent family history would prove, the 22-year-old Robert junior would prove a worthy successor to his father. He built upon the foundations laid and established the Shaw family as one of Dublin's leading banking and political families of the first half of the 19th century.

The banking system in 18th-century Ireland was fairly haphazard and unreliable, characterized by regular bank failures generally as a consequence of poor harvests, fraud and overtrading. Hall maintained that 'Generally speaking, however, the commercial morality of professional bankers at this period was at a very low ebb'.[25] Powell described the banking community in even-less flattering terms when commenting on the private banker's capacity to issue bank notes he wrote that 'every grocer, draper, tailor and haberdasher who chose might flood the country with their rags.'[26]

Banks in the late 18th century were very different from modern banks. Until the 1820s most were what was termed private banks. The term 'private bank' referred to the ownership structure. Banks in the 18th century were generally owned by merchants or land agents who had good working capital and profit reserves and saw the opportunities these presented. Most were undercapitalized and many over-expanded their lending base which meant that, when the inevitable liquidity pressures arose, there was a spate of bank failures. Given Ireland's dependence on the income from agriculture and land in general, poor harvests and weak markets for exports such as linen and cattle, it is not surprising to observe that most of the banking crises that occurred did so when agricultural fortunes declined. Poor banking practices, and in many instances downright fraud, also contributed significantly to bank collapses.

Banking functions during the 18th and 19th centuries were relatively limited. In the main, they included the issuance of bank notes, issuing and discounting bills of exchange, receiving deposits and advancing loans usually by way of a mortgage on property. Up until the advent of joint stock banks in the second quarter of the 19th century, banks could only operate within narrowly defined geographic areas. The owners of each bank had to live in the area where the bank conducted its business. This meant that outside of the metropolitan centres of Dublin, Cork and Belfast, there were few banking facilities. A consequence of this was that local issues such as the bankruptcy of a local merchant or a flooding of a particular town, gave rise to failures. Given that banks were not limited liability companies, collapse meant total ruin for the owners with the result that failures were often followed by suicides, absconding from the jurisdiction or long sojourns in various debtors' prisons.

At the time of the founding of Bank of Ireland in 1783, the four leading private banks in the country were David La Touche & Sons, William Gleadowe & Co., Thomas Finlay & Co. and Coates & Lawless. Interestingly the proprietors of all these banks were initial subscribers in the share capital of Bank of Ireland and most were either directors, governors or deputy governors of the bank in its early years. As a consequence the relationship between the newly founded bank and its competitors was cordial and supportive. This situation was to change when David La Touche stood down as the bank's first governor in the mid-1790s and it started to take a more hostile attitude to what it perceived as competition.

The prosperity brought about by the good agricultural income as a result of the Napoleonic wars, the development of the newly independent Americas and the consequent domestic building boom on great estate and city houses proved very fertile ground for private banks. Growth in the opening years of the 19th century was dramatic. In 1800 there were 11 private banks in Ireland while by 1804 this had risen to 40.[27]

It was in this environment that Robert Shaw junior, following the death of his father in 1796, appears to have decided to formalize the family's involvement in the banking business. His decision is likely to have been helped by his marriage in the same year to Maria Wilkinson, the only daughter and heiress of Abraham Wilkinson of Mount Jerome, Dublin. Apart from a dowry of £10,000, the marriage brought with it ownership of two significant houses and estates in the Terenure and Crumlin areas of Dublin: Bushy Park House and Kimmage Manor. His wife's father was a wealthy Dublin merchant and landowner, and was extremely well connected in business and political circles. Like Robert's father he was an original subscriber to Bank of Ireland at its foundation and was a deputy and subsequent governor of the bank. From entries in the account books of Robert Shaw & Son, it appears that Wilkinson had dealings with the firm. For instance, an entry dated 11 August 1786 shows 'By bill 484 Abraham Wilkinson note to Ben Loftus £20'.[28] Clearly the exposure did not provide any negative impressions as Wilkinson deemed the young Robert to be a suitable husband for his only and presumably beloved daughter.

Milne in his *History of the Royal Bank of Ireland* tells us that 'February 20 1867 was a bad day for the historian of the Royal Bank of Ireland', for, so the Board minutes tell us, 'due to congestion in the safe all letters and papers that bore dates prior to 1846 were ordered to be destroyed forthwith.'[29] With this decision much, if not all, of the internal workings of the Robert Shaw Bank were lost to posterity.

The genesis of the family's involvement in formal banking was the establishment by Sir Thomas Lighton of a private bank at 78 Fleet Street in 1796. The property was owned by Robert Shaw senior.[30] Lighton, from Strabane, was a former mercenary for the East India Tea Company, who made his money by providing safe passage for his commanding officer's widow and fortune back to England, following the officer's being taken prisoner by a warring tribe and eventually murdered. He was also MP for Tuam, and eventually Carlingford. In 1799 he transferred the business around the corner to 4 Foster Place from where the bank's various successors in title continued in business down to the late 1990s when AIB vacated it. More significantly a new partnership was established involving Lighton, Thomas Needham of Lucan and Robert Shaw. The bank was known as The Lighton, Needham and Shaw Bank.

In 1805, Lighton died and the partnership was reconstituted between Needham and Shaw. This situation continued up until 1817 when the partnership was extended to include Shaw's younger brother Ponsonby. According to Milne, each of the three partners contributed £20,000 equity.[31]

The timing of this new funding arrangement is significant, coming as it did in a period of relative economic downturn following the ending of the Napoleonic wars and at a time of significant land agitation. The partnership was again renewed on its tenth anniversary in 1827. Following Shaw's elevation to baronet in 1821, the bank was simply known as the Sir Robert Shaw Bank, and operated under this name until it eventually metamorphosed itself into the Royal Bank of Ireland in 1836, when it converted from private to joint stock status.

3 Logo of the Lighton, Needham, Shaw Bank

Like all private banks of the time, the Robert Shaw Bank encountered many difficulties. As a private bank one of its chief functions and entitlements was the issuing of bank notes. The fact that upwards of 40 private banks could issue notes in a relatively unregulated and uncontrolled way could, and did, give rise to all sorts of abuses. Some of these were exercises in poor financial judgment or recklessness, while for others the temptation to 'print money' proved too strong. Another abuse related to the forging of bank notes and as the following notice that appeared in the *Freeman's Journal* highlights, the Shaw Bank was not immune from this threat:

> Reward of £100 and £50
>
> Robert Shaw, Esq. and Co. will give a reward of £100 Sterling, to any person or persons who will prosecute to conviction, the person or persons who engraved the copper-plates of, or signed the names to, any of the notes lately forged on their Bank. And they will pay a further reward of £50 sterling, to any person or persons who will prosecute to conviction any of the persons employed to pass and have passed into circulation any of such forgeries:
>
> Foster Place, December 20, 1811.[32]

Embodying the requisite skills and characteristics of a banker in the 19th century, namely, probity, soundness, social skills and personal contacts, Robert Shaw led a thriving bank into the economic boom of the early 1800s. Furthermore, when crises hit, as they did in 1814 and particularly in 1820, it would appear that the bank had both sufficient financial and reputational

capital built up to weather the storms, albeit with support from Bank of
Ireland, which was by then assuming the responsibilities of a central bank in
terms of 'lender of last resort' facilities. Not that approaches to the Bank were
welcomed or made easy. Hall describes the situation in 1820 when the Shaw's
Bank approached Bank of Ireland for short-term facilities to tide them over
a particularly difficult period:

> On the 12th June when the storm broke in Dublin, considerable
> excitement prevailed. The Court [of the Bank of Ireland] was in
> continuous session all day ... Later in the day all the Dublin private
> bankers applied for assistance. An application by Shaws Bank, to discount
> a total amount of £50,000 in bills and for an advance of £11,000 on
> the security of Government stock was the first to be considered.
> Apparently this concern had received accommodation to the extent of
> £100,000 during a period of pressure that had occurred in the year 1814,
> and on that occasion the partners of the firm had given an undertaking
> that in future the business would be kept within the level of their
> resources. Accordingly Leland Crosthwait and Goff were sent to
> interview the principals of Shaws Bank, and to remind them of the
> promise they had previously given. The partners of Shaws Bank assured
> these directors that the application now made represented the full extent
> of their requirements, and that this accommodation was needed purely
> on account of the crisis. The Court again reconsidered the matter, and
> in view of the urgency of the circumstances it was decided to grant the
> application.[33]

With the support of Bank of Ireland, Shaws Bank was one of only 15 of the
31 private banks in existence at the start of 1820 to survive the crisis brought
about by a severe drop in farm commodity prices.

A contemporary extract from the diary of James Digges (La Touche)
captures the mood and sense of panic that was felt by all bankers of the day.

> We heard of the stoppage of two Cork banks, Messers Leslie and Messers
> Roche. We heard it as the sound of distant thunder ... but with the idea
> that it little affected us. The Monday following we learned the failure
> of Messers Maunsells of Limerick and, on Wednesday, that of Messers
> Bruce and Co. of Limerick and Charleville had also stopped payment.
> A violent run on all the country banks also took place ... My mind,
> naturally nervous and timid, foreboded evil ... frightful dreams disturbed
> my rest at night; and by day the phantom of uncertain evil haunted my
> path. The scriptures and some of Leighton's works came with
> inexpressible power to the soul ... 'in the time of trouble I sought the

Lord' … Still … the danger … was at a distance. The stability of Messers Riall of Clonmel seemed to tranquilize the public mind, and to guard Dublin from evil. But … we learned … on Thursday that Messrs Riall's Bank had been obliged to stop payment. The failure of Alexanders Bank … on the ensuing Monday directed suspicion towards Dublin, and a run commenced on the Dublin Banks which, however, they all sustained … But the Lord graciously put a bound to the progress of His judgments. He chastened us and corrected us; but blessed be His name … He kept my mind in peace.[34]

The crisis exposed the inherent weaknesses of the private banks, namely poor capitalization, localized activities, inability to raise equity due to restrictions on ownership and poor control and regulation. It proved to be a turning-point in terms of their continued existence. While some, like the mighty La Touche Bank, did continue in business for some years to come, it too collapsed in 1870; not one private bank survived the century.

The advent of joint stock banks following the enactment of various Banking Acts, in the immediate aftermath of the 1820 crisis, was designed to place banking on a sounder footing. Joint stock banks could raise capital from a wider base than heretofore and operate a branch network and for the first time allowed for a separation of ownership and management. The banks set up in this period such as the Provincial (1825), the Hibernian (1825), the National (1834), the Royal (1836), the Belfast (1827) and the Ulster (1836) were to change the face of banking in Ireland and to continue up until the 1960s when most were merged to form the AIB and the Bank of Ireland groups.

Unlike his great rivals, the La Touches, Robert Shaw must have recognized this trend as he was the main driver behind the formation of the Royal Bank of Ireland with which he merged the Sir Robert Shaw Bank. Interestingly neither Robert nor indeed any family member became directors in the Royal Bank on its formation or at any subsequent time. The reason for this is unclear, although it may have been due to the fact that he, Robert, was 62 and was spending most of his time in London, having married his second wife Amelia Spencer there in 1834. The fact also that none of his offspring appear to have been interested in business may have contributed to his seeking an orderly exit from the business. Regardless of the motivation, Sir Robert's retirement from the firm appears to have ended the family's involvement in banking and commerce in general.

However, occasional newspaper references provide evidence of involvement in a number of ventures, ranging from an insurance company based in 40 Dame Street under the title of The British and Irish United Fire Insurance Company to the peculiarly named Raper's Waterproof Manufacture

Company.[35] The former venture also involved five members of the La Touche family whose history displayed many similarities to the Shaws in that both families came to Ireland in 1690 with the Williamite army, both were awarded lands for their services to William III, both established themselves as prominent merchants, both had family as MPs in the College Green Parliament, both became prominent bankers and both were prominent families in Dublin society of the late 18th and 19th centuries. While the Shaws were the relatively poor relations, given the striking similarities it is distinctly possible that the La Touches acted as role models for the first Robert Shaw of Terenure. In the same vein it is likely that there was a rivalry, particularly as the Shaws were becoming successful, although no concrete evidence has come to light to prove this contention.

Sir Robert also was the driving force behind the establishment of the General Cemetery Company of Dublin in 1836.[36] The main activity of this company was the purchase of the lands of Mount Jerome in Harold's Cross from the earl of Meath for the purpose of opening and operating a burial ground for Dublin Protestants. Shaw was joined by Sydney Herbert (Herbert Park and Street) and Robert Gray, who was credited with bringing a clean water supply to Dublin. The site which is now the current Mount Jerome cemetery had coincidentally been the home of Sir Robert's father-in-law, Abraham Wilkinson.

While later members of the family may well have gone into business as partners or principals none of them achieved anything like the prominence or success of the first two Roberts of Terenure. With the merging of the family bank into the Royal Bank the Shaw name all but disappeared from the business life of Dublin although the family name remained prominent in terms of politics, public administration and as landowners in the city and county.

2. Accumulators, consolidators and spenders, 1786–1876

In April 1876, just three months before his death, Frederick Shaw, third baronet, the then family patriarch, was listed in the Local Government Board's *Return of the owners of land in Ireland* as the owner of 996 acres, 2 roods and 30 perches in Dublin with an annual valuation of £2,974.[1] This made him one of the top 30 landlords in the county alongside land barons such as the Pembrokes, Talbots, Domvilles and the earl of Howth. Only one other Shaw, his brother, William, is listed, implying that Frederick was the custodian of the family estates in Terenure, Crumlin, Tallaght and beyond. While it may not have been obvious at the time, the family's fortunes had reached their zenith and were henceforth in decline. Between that point and a time some one hundred years earlier, when a young Robert started his flour merchant business, can be charted the rise of an upper middle-class family and their elevation to the highest social and political circles of Dublin life.

Typical of similar entrepreneurial families in the industrializing world, it is a story of dynamic and energetic early generations followed by scions less driven by the need to enhance the family's fortunes and who were more focused on lifestyle and discovering meaning in life. The four patriarchal figures in this story are to a greater or lesser extent representative of points in a family life cycle incorporating as they do accumulators, consolidators and spenders of a clan's fortune.

The early family account books reveal a story of drive, skilled financial management, business acumen, and a network of social and political contacts that were necessary if one were to succeed in commercial life. The account books also illustrate a clear demarcation between the business and family finances. Like the account books covered in the previous chapter the books are meticulously maintained and indicate a significant number of transactions. Given the notation and handwriting they appear to have been written up by Robert Shaw himself. An interesting observation is that the vast majority of the transactions represent cash disbursements to individuals and there is little evidence of any borrowings by the family to finance these advances. This can only mean that there were separate account books, not in the family paper collection, for borrowings (which from an accounting perspective would be unusual) or more likely that the family had sufficient independent sources of funds most probably from the profits of the merchant and bond holding business. If the latter assumption is correct than it must have been a highly profitable business indeed. It is also another example of the family carrying on a quasi-banking activity or as it might otherwise be described, a money lending business.

The accounts also reveal Shaw as a very astute and conservative investor. While there are some references to share dealing, which was an increasingly popular form of investment in the late 18th century as evidenced, for example, by the fact that the New York Stock Exchange was established in 1792 and was followed in 1801 by London as a means of providing regulated markets for dealing in shares, such activity on the part of the Shaws was relatively limited. The account books show that, from an investment perspective, Shaw was clearly attracted to developing future income streams rather than seeking speculative capital gains.

One of the most popular types of investment was the purchase of rights to all or part of a client's pension entitlements, to judge, for instance, from entries dated 21 July 1786 and 1 November 1791 illustrating the type of transactions he involved himself in:

> Purchase from the Honorable John Burke a further annuity of £250 a year at four years purchase to commence from 2nd June last – £1,000.

> Owen O'Connor Esq. of Milltown, near Castlerea, in half his pay as lieutenant in Lord Shahavens corp at the pay office in London. £44 19s. 6d. for 5 years purchased at £224 17s. 6d.[2]

The first transaction above would have no doubt come about as a result of Mr Burke needing to raise £1,000 of capital for some purpose or other, and to do so he was prepared to sell on his entitlement to £250 worth of pension for the remainder of his life. From Shaw's perspective should Burke have lived longer than four years then he would be in profit, whereas if he were to die prior to four years he would lose out on the transaction. However, as a subsequent entry makes clear, Shaw managed effectively to hedge his position by taking out an insurance policy on the life of the person selling the interest. Thus if the individual were to die within the four years, the policy proceeds would cover his outlay. Shaw also engaged in the purchase of annuities derived from patents as the following entry from 6 September 1786 illustrates:

> Purchase of William Hamilton of £1,750 patent income to be distributed to
> – Robert Shaw junior   £800
> – Bernard Shaw   £700
> – Mary Shaw   £250
> The price paid to represent 8.5 years purchase – £14,038 16s. 3d.[3]

There are a number of issues raised by the above entry. Firstly, he was dealing on a substantial scale in that the purchase price of £14,038 would represent approximately £1.7 million in 2009 terms.[4] The second issue is that a flow of patent income is significantly more valuable than a flow of pension income, hence the much higher multiple paid of eight and a half years' purchase, compared to four times for the earlier mentioned transaction. This of course is no doubt due to the longer potential life of the income source, usually twenty years. The third and most significant aspect from this story's standpoint is that he is, in this instance, purchasing the income streams on behalf of his children. At the time of this particular transaction in 1786, Robert Shaw was still a young man of 37, and the approach he adopted in providing for his children is a clear exercise in good estate planning, demonstrating significant forethought. Providing for his children in this way is in stark contrast to the way many of the landed families did through borrowing on their estates. Shaw displayed further financial engineering skills when putting in place a hedge, by taking out insurance policies on each of the three children's lives at the same time, as the following entry illustrates:

Purchase from Royal Exchange Insurance at an annual cost of £194 11s. 10d.,

– Robert Shaw junior	£3,500
– Bernard Shaw	£3,000
– Mary Shaw	£2,000[5]

In the same year of this transaction, 1786, Shaw took a lease on Terenure House, from a fellow Kilkenny man, Joseph Deane.[6] The signing of the lease, which covered a house (now Terenure College) and 40 acres at prices ranging from £10 to £6 per acre, marked the beginning of the family's 166-year long association with the Terenure area. It also represented an extraordinary progression for Shaw who was now in a position to afford a substantial city residence in fashionable Fleet Street and also a mansion in the county where his young family could grow in a healthy and idyllic environment.

Many of the entries record significant personal loans advanced to members of the aristocracy, for example the earls of Bellmont, Glandore, Hillsborough and numerous lesser peers. An example of this type of transaction can be seen in the following entries dated 18 June 1790: 'Earl of Bellmont lent him on his own bond £5,000' and again on 8 April 1791 'Lent him further £5,000 on his own bond at 6% interest'.[7] The account books also show a number of entries whereby he advanced loans to various extended family members such as his father-in-law, Joseph Higgins, his brothers, Thomas and William, and his maternal uncle, George Markham. Interestingly in all these transactions there is a degree of formality in terms of legal charges being taken and bonds being entered into.

4 Terenure House *c.*1800

While, as previously mentioned, the Shaws were substantial land and property owners, it is clear from the evidence that unlike many of the landed estate class they had little emotional attachment to land. Instead, they saw land as simply an asset class which could be bought and sold like any other form of investment. The way entries are recorded in the account books makes this clear. We see this in the purchase of a farm in an entry dated 7 March 1786:

> Farm of Carrickmines purchased of Mr Thomas Parker being a lease from the dean and chapter Christchurch for 21 years and renewable as usual. Set during the life of Edmund Beasley of Glasnevin. The lease to commence to me 25th March 1785 at £79 18s. payable by William Allen. Paid £1,077 10s. at 13.5 years purchase price.[8]

An entry dated April 1790 substantiates a previously uncorroborated story that Shaw had acquired a significant estate near the old family seat in Thomastown:

> Purchase of the Thomastown estate from Eland Massom Esq., 29th September 1790, balance paid 13th April 1791 £2,000 – half yearly rent £487 3s. 7d. Annual profit rent £504 17s. 7d.[9]

This property was subsequently sold in 1821 by his son Robert, to the earl of Carrick when he was assembling the Mount Juliet Estate.

Tenant	Property	Term of Lease	Rent
Henry Casson	One large house recently built	31 years from 1771	£40
Edward Mc Alister/ Tobin	One house and the Liberty crane	53 years from 1788	£15
Matthew Garonly	The Gaster Inn, stables, coach house, dwelling house and gardens	31 years from 25th Mar 1782	£60
James Mooney	Two houses	31 year lease from 29th Sept 1783	£60
Daniel Fearon	Five houses – 3 of them built by himself	56 year lease from 29th Sept 1784	£62
Martin Fitzgerald	4 houses	56 year lease from 29th Sept 1784	£45
Martin Fitzgerald	Large stables and yard	53 years from 29th Sept 1788	£20
Ejected Mrs Mc Cabe - Street woman	2 houses	56 year lease from 29th Dec 1784	£26
James Thompson	1 house	52 year lease from 29th Sept 1784	£26
James Rooney	The Sheaf Inn and stables	56 year lease from 29th Sept 1784	£30
Thompson x John Kearns	2 houses	55 year lease from 24th Jun 1785	£30
Sylvester Byrne	1 house and stable	56 year lease from 24th Jun 1785	£18
John James	1 house	No lease	£10
Widow of John Gallagher	1 house	No lease	£10[10]

An illustration that the property asset class did not just extend to farmland but included residential and commercial interests as well can be seen in a number of entries relating to the purchase of houses in Dublin city. One in particular that provides a good insight into the rents people paid for houses and business premises is dated September 1788:

Purchased of George Allery a holding on the south and east side of
Kevin Street being a lease from the Vicars Choral of St Patrick's cathedral
for 60 years from 25th March 1783. There was then fifty-five years to
run on the lease and the renewal fine was £200. The usual mode is for
the Choral to renew every 15 years. Paid Mr Allery £3,500. Yearly rent
paid by the tenants £420 less Choral head rent £15 17s. 6d. giving an
annual profit rent of £404 12s. 6d. Tenants.

Apart from the purchase price and the level of rents for various properties, the
information contained in the entry indicates that leases on residential and
commercial properties were of a significantly longer duration than modern
leases.

The records also show Shaw purchasing shares, although it should be noted
that such transactions are few relative to the purchase of annuities or properties.
Examples of share transactions see Shaw buying four shares of £500 per share
in the Ship Insurance Company. In keeping with his investment philosophy
he refers to the dividend being £32 per annum. Seven years later we see him
buying a further four shares in the name of his son Robert for £425 per share
and the dividend is stated to be £25 per annum. On 24 June 1792 there is an
interesting entry relating to an investment in the Royal Canal Company:

Royal Canal Company. The company having granted an annuity of
£200 as a premium for the loan of £30,000 at 4 per cent taken jointly
by Sir William Newcommen and myself. I bought off Sir William half
of the annuity of £100 pa for 16 years purchase. The whole annuity is
therefore mine and the lives named are Priscilla Cecilia Shaw my wife,
Charollote my second daughter born 9th April 1792. The annuity
commences 24th June 1792. Paid £1,600.[11]

The account books show a bewildering array of transactions being carried
on by Robert Shaw. Given the geographic spread of the counter-parties
involved he clearly had established a nationwide reputation as a man of
discretion, substance and honour. That one individual could engage in so many
transactions and on such a scale, while at the same time running a successful
merchanting and bond holding business, is testimony to his abilities and
financial capability and is the main reason for the family's wealth and status
over the next two centuries. Not surprisingly, Shaw's domestic and commercial
responsibilities, which he took very seriously allowed little time for
engagement with the Dublin social scene. We know that he was a member of
the Freemasons, joining the 137th Dublin Lodge in 1781 which is likely to
have involved him in charitable works but of these little is known.[12] Allowing
for the usual elegiac hyperbole his obituary made reference to his devotion to
work:

From too great an attention to, and anxiety about business (not solely for his own emolument) and neglecting to take the salutary relaxation necessary to preserve the human frame in health, Mr Shaw had for many months labored under a complaint which had too natural a tendency to sudden and fatal issue and so it happened.[13]

The obituary also gave an insight into the respect in which he was held by many citizens of Dublin:

Thousands, who were not personally acquainted with the late Robert Shaw, will regret his death, because it was a public loss – because he was the benevolent citizen of the world, whose mind unfettered by any selfish, narrow prejudices studied to be useful to mankind.

Clearly inheriting his father's business acumen, ambition and drive, Robert Shaw (the subsequent first baronet) who graduated from Trinity College Dublin with a BA in 1792, started in the family flour merchanting business. Within four years, at the age of 22, he had, as described in the previous chapter, formalized the family's financial dealings through the foundation of the Lighton, Needham and Shaw Bank. Because of the destruction of the records of this bank's business dealings, one does not have an opportunity of gaining insight into the first baronet's investment practices or the drawings he made from the business. What we do know, however, is that the mainstay of the family's land portfolio was as a direct consequence of his marriage to Maria Wilkinson, the only child and heiress of her father Abraham Wilkinson. Wilkinson was a wealthy Dublin merchant and property owner. On her marriage to Robert, Maria received a substantial dowry consisting of £10,000 in cash and the not-insignificant additions of two mansions and related estates in Terenure and nearby Crumlin. The Terenure estate consisted of Bushy Park House and approximately 110 acres of land bordering the river Dodder, and extending from Templeogue to Terenure village. The Kimmage estate as described by Frederick Shaw in 1858 consisted of Kimmage House (Kimmage Manor is presently a seminary/training college for the Holy Ghost Fathers order) and approximately 500 statute acres made up of a number of distinct and separate farms.[14] Bushy Park became the family seat for the next 156 years while the Crumlin estate was to remain in the family up until 1877.

Robert, the first baronet, displayed remarkable energy across a whole range of areas. As a business man he became a highly successful banker, as a politician he bestrode both the local and national stages for over thirty years, and as a member of society he was an integral part of the Dublin social scene, championing a range of social causes. When he was 58 he re-entered Trinity College and obtained an MA. He fathered eight children who survived to adulthood with his first wife Maria. Following the death of his first wife he

5 Bushy Park House *c.*1800

married Amelia Spencer in London in 1834. Taking up almost permanent residence in London, the couple were highly instrumental in founding the Twickenham United Reformed Church.[15]

While displaying similar industry to his father, Robert junior appears to have been more comfortable in maintaining a higher public profile, whether it was in business, politics or Dublin's social life. As mentioned above the records of his bank were destroyed in 1846, and it is not clear if it was by accident or design that the financial records of the merchanting business and the family account books during his tenure in charge are not part of the significant volume of family papers available to us. However, the deficit in financial records is compensated for by a welter of references to Robert junior's attendance at various social gatherings and involvement with various charitable causes, of which the following are examples:

Grand Entertainment at the Mansion House
The Right Hon. the Lord Mayor of Dublin had the honor of entertaining his Excellency the Lord-Lieutenant and a distinguished company at theMansion House yesterday evening ... Amongst the distinguished guests were The Lord Chancellor, the Chief Secretary of State, Sir Robert Shaw ...[16]

Coronation Dinner

Yesterday evening this grand public festival took place in Morrisson's Great Rooms, the Right Honorable, the Lord Mayor in the chair, the earl of Fingall, Vice President – and a day more worthy to be remembered has never occurred in the history of this country. It was most delightful to witness upwards of four hundred Protestant and Catholic gentlemen, sitting down together at the festive board, in the utmost harmony and cordiality, who before had been alienated from each other by party feelings and party misconceptions, and at once forgetting all their animosities and disputes in one universal sentiment of devotion to the Sovereign, of affection to the country and of peace and goodwill towards each other. Among the attendees were … Robert Shaw.[17]

While the family attained most of its wealth through the efforts of the first Robert of Terenure it was through his son Robert that they achieved much of their social status. From the time he became a member of the soon to be abolished Irish Parliament in 1799 as MP for Bannow, he was destined to hold many important public positions such as high sheriff of the city of Dublin (1797), sheriff for Co. Dublin (1806), alderman for Dublin (1808), MP to the Imperial Parliament (1804–26) and lord mayor of Dublin (1815–16). However, the crowning glory for his family and himself, came in 1821 when, following the coronation of George IV, he was created a baronet, a title which the family bear to this day.

Like his father, Sir Robert, the first baronet enjoyed an excellent public reputation and was clearly held to be an honorable and capable man by family members and business associates. This is evident in the number of estates to which he was appointed executor. One of the more interesting ones subsequently gave rise to a most enduring literary character, when immortalized by the family's most famous descendant, George Bernard Shaw, in his play, *Pygmalion*:

Indenture made the [blank] day of [blank] in the year of our Lord one thousand eight hundred and twenty three between Eliza Doolittle of the city of Cork, spinster of the first part, Isabella Doolittle of the said city of Cork, spinster of the second part, Henry Doolittle of Bridge Street in the city of Dublin, merchant of the third part and Sir Robert Shaw of Bushy Park in the county of Dublin, baronet, executor of the last will and testament of Lydia Wilkinson spinster, deceased of the fourth part.[18]

Given Sir Robert's involvement in business and politics, as well as his domestic role as a father of eight children, the array of committees on which he served is remarkable. He was an active member of the Royal Dublin Society, a magistrate of Rathfarnham Court, treasurer of the female school of Tallaght, president of the Seminary for the General and Polite Education Gardiner Street, trustee of the Charitable Society for the Relief of Sick and Indigent Roomkeepers, treasurer of the Dorset Institution of Lower Abbey Street, chairman for the Day School for the Instruction of Young Gentlemen, church warden St Andrew's parish, governor of the Hospital for Incurables in Donnybrook and treasurer of the Lord Mayor's Committee for Relief of the Poor.[19]

It is interesting that, on many of the committees on which he served, Sir Robert was regularly joined by members of the La Touche, Newcommen, Lee, Pim and Darley families. It is clear that in contrast to the prevailing political doctrine of *laissez faire* there was a strong sense of a duty of care among many of the Dublin middle class towards the less fortunate. This theme of *noblesse oblige* was characteristic of middle classes throughout Europe and the United States of America. It was a concept enshrined within the Protestant churches and even many of the societies of the day; for instance, a Masonic handbook from 1759 instructed its members 'to be submissive to superiors, courteous and affable to equals, and kind and condescending to inferiors'.[20]

If the first two Roberts of our story could be said to be driven, ambitious and the generators of wealth, the same cannot be said of the third Robert, second baronet. Unlike his father and his younger brother Frederick, he did not engage in representative politics. Nor does he appear to demonstrate any of the entrepreneurial flair that was such a characteristic of his father's and grandfather's careers. We know from *Pigot's directory* that, like his grandfather, he held the position of Accountant General of the Irish Post Office.[21] However, based on his diary entries, the post does not seem to have been all that demanding of his time as instanced by an entry dated Monday, 1 March 1824 which records:

> Rose early, breakfasted at the Kildare Street Club. Went to the Post Office, stayed there till past three. Walked about with Lord Clarina till dinner time. Dined at Ms Lawlesses, music there in the evening. Afterwards went to Mrs Grealy's. Slept at the Hibernian Hotel, Dawson Street.[22]

Interestingly, his diary entries for the remainder of that week make no reference to him attending the 'Post Office'.

The second baronet was born in 1796. He never married, and his diary entries which cover the period 1824 to 1836, make no references to him being in a relationship with anyone. Many of the entries refer to his interest in religion, and indeed one of his community involvements was with a Sunday school which he appeared to be instrumental in running. For example his entry for Sunday, 14 March 1824 records, 'Went to the Sunday school, after one of the boys in my class told me he could not come anymore. I suspect the priest at Harold's Cross has forbidden him to attend longer.'[23]

While the Shaws had always been noted supporters of the Established Church and hostile to many of the Catholic causes, the second baronet appears to have been particularly virulent in his attitude. For instance his last will and testament, dated 21 January 1862, contains a clause which stipulates that, should any of the beneficiaries to his will, ever become Roman Catholics, then they, and any of their lineal descendants, will be disinherited.[24]

In this context it is ironic that diary entries relating to a visit to Rome in 1836 record, 'High mass performed by the Pope at St Peters. The sight was very grand. Afterwards the blessing was given in a most imposing manner by the Pope in front of the church.' An entry a few days later on 19 April shows him meeting the Pope in person, 'Was introduced to the Pope by Comite de Grice. Had some conversation with him. He recommended that I call upon [name indecipherable] and bring him his compliments.'[25]

It would be easy to conclude from their attitude that they were a bigoted family. This may have indeed been the case, but their attitudes were probably representative of the mood of the time, among not just the ruling elite, but also the Protestant community in general. It is not to difficult to understand why this would have been the case. Having controlled and governed Ireland for well over two hundred years the first inklings of a Catholic response were being felt and the Protestant minority would undoubtedly have seen themselves under threat from those whom they would see as inferior. Given the threat to their way of life it is easy to understand how they would be hostile to the Catholic community. In this sense the family were not in anyway unusual in their attitudes.

Travel appears to have featured prominently in the second baronet's life. For instance, his diary entries for 1830 refer to a six-week tour of the Cumberland lakes and Scotland with his two sisters, Lydia and Charlotte, when he was 34, substantiating the earlier view expressed, that unlike his father and grandfather, he had little to do with commerce. He also seems to have enjoyed socializing with the upper echelons of both Irish and English society as the following entry from 15 February 1836 indicates: 'Breakfasted at the Carlton Club. Wrote letters. Made preparation for journey [a seven-month tour of France, Austria and Italy]. Dined with the duke and duchess of Leinster'.[26]

The entries show a close-knit family with regular get togethers and dinner engagements. One from Monday 23 August reads, 'Left Bushy Park with my sisters Lydia and Charlotte … We dined at three; my father, mother and all the family came down to see us off. We sailed at six on the Emerald Isle to Liverpool.'[27]

He also had a keen interest in gardening and indeed the running of the Bushy Park estate. For instance, the entries for a whole week in March 1826 record his activities in the garden and indeed on his return after the aforementioned six-week tour of the lakes and Scotland in 1830, his diary states 'Reached home at four. We found all our friends well and the garden looking very gay.'[28] That he could afford to lead the life he did was due in the main to his control of the Bushy Park estate. An interesting feature is that he appears to have taken the estate under the terms of the will of his maternal grandfather, Abraham Wilkinson. As his own will states 'known as my Terenure Estate and so called and designated in a map now in my possession and as same are designated therein and to which I became entitled under the will of my grandfather the late Abraham Wilkinson Esq.'[29]

The primacy of the first born son is borne out by his mother's will dated 2 February 1809, when having left some relatively minor bequests to some charities and strangely just to one of her daughters, she wills to Robert 'all I shall die possessed of with my blessing and prayer that they may be a blessing to his children and the world.'[30]

He appears to have had control of the estate for some time prior to the death of his father in 1849. Robert, first baronet, had moved to his town house on Merrion Square and then since the death of his first wife Maria, was spending more of his time in London, where as previously stated, he met and married his second wife, Amelia Spencer, in 1834. Whether his father's vacating of the Bushy Park estate was for financial reasons or otherwise is not evident, although the domestic account books maintained by Robert, second baronet, for the period 1822–31, show almost monthly entries referring to '£80 payment to my father'.[31] His father's last will and testament makes indirect reference to the earlier passing of the estates to his sons Robert and Frederick, when having left amounts of up to £5,000 to each of his other children he left £50 to them with the comment 'he being already so well provided for'.[32]

In drafting his will, Sir Robert, first baronet, clearly recognized the possibility of at least one of his children disputing the will when he provided that:

> I hereby declare it to be my will that in case any of my children shall hereafter dispute or challenge any of the foregoing dispositions in this my will with respect to … I hereby revoke the bequest or bequests hereinbefore made in favour of such child or children so disputing or questioning same and in lieu thereof I hereby bequeath onto such child or children so disputing or questioning said dispositions the sum of £10 sterling each and I wish and direct that the remainder of the sum or sums so hereinbefore bequeathed to such child or children be equally divided among the remainder of my children who shall not dispute or question any of the foregoing dispositions.[33]

Another interesting aspect of Robert's will was the bequest to his second wife, Amelia: 'I leave to my dear wife Amelia Shaw, nee Spencer, my carriage and

6 Frederick Shaw

a pair of horses, she making her choice of what carriage and horses she may wish to keep'.

The family account books, which are again meticulously maintained, provide insight into both the lifestyle and character of the second baronet and the costs associated with running a relatively small estate like Terenure. For instance salaries for most of the ten years covered by the accounts ran at £125 per quarter or £500 per annum which when one considers annual rents for an albeit later period, 1869, totaling £2,936 (Appendix 2), indicate a highly profitable venture.[34] The rents allowed the second baronet to fund his many foreign trips, pay his barber 6s. 8d. per week, purchase ball tickets for £10, pay subscriptions to the Carlton and Kildare Street Clubs and spend several hundred pounds a year on buying clothes from his London tailor. They also show his generous spirit with numerous entries recording 'payments to a poor man 5s. or to a poor woman 10s.' or an entry dated July 1824 'my barber – lent him £6 16s. 2d.'[35]

Robert, second baronet, lieutenant colonel of the Dublin militia, succeeded to his father's title on his death in 1849. He was 53 years old and was to retain the title for twenty years until his death in 1869, when it passed to his younger brother, Frederick, who was 70 when he succeeded. Interestingly, when he died there were no obituaries in the national papers. The only obvious reference to his death was in the notices of the Royal Horticultural Society of Ireland that appeared in the *Irish Times* and *Daily Advertiser* of 12 November 1869 which noted:

> It is with no ordinary regret that your council have to deplore the demise of their colleague and chairman the late Sir Robert Shaw, Bart. One of the very earlier members of your society and for a long series of years an active member of its executive, he at all times and under all circumstances evinced the liveliest interest in its working and welfare. Affable, kind and conciliatory, he possessed no ordinary degree of those qualities which, always exercised for your advantage, were alike calculated to disarm opposition and to win support.[36]

Frederick, three years his brother's junior, appears to have led a more industrious life than his older sibling. He married Thomasine Emily Jocelyn in 1819 when he was only 20 years of age and still studying for a BA at Brasenose College, Oxford.[37] After university, he studied law and was called to the Irish bar in 1822. He was clearly successful in his legal career because by 1826 he was appointed recorder for Dundalk and two years later he was made recorder for Dublin. He was appointed attorney general in November 1834.[38] Like his father he represented Dublin City and later Dublin University in the Westminster Parliament. As we will see in the following chapter he was the most politically accomplished of the family. Apart from the running of his Crumlin estate he does not appear to have involved himself in commerce. His wife, Thomasine, to whom he was married for 40 years and with whom he had six children, was the daughter of the Honourable George Jocelyn and granddaughter of the first earl of Roden, founder of the Orange Order.

Little appears in the ubiquitous social and personal columns concerning Frederick's involvement with the Dublin social scene. An insight into life on the Crumlin estate and its house, Kimmage House, can be gleaned from the biography of Flora Shaw, his granddaughter, who was the first female correspondent of *The Times* and whose husband Lord Frederick Lugard was the Governor of Nigeria. She paints a picture of an idyllic setting watched over by a caring and loving patriarch:

> Shaw was a rather formidable grandfather with his great dignity and old fashioned courtesy. He expected of children a high standard of manners and consideration, but he was invariably patient and gentle with them and his rebukes were embodied in stories which carried a relevant moral. As they grew older and were able to become to some extent his companions, they learnt much from his conversation and example; they acquired a high sense of responsibility which belongs to the privileged,

of the duty of generous service. 'It's the privilege of a gentleman' he would say, 'to get the worst of any bargain throughout life'.[39]

Frederick was plagued by ill health in that he suffered from severe rheumatism. The illness forced his retirement from representative politics and is said to have prevented him accepting the role of lord lieutenant of Ireland from Prime Minister Robert Peel in 1834.[40] Interestingly in a letter dated 23 December 1834, from Peel to Shaw, we see a degree of familiarity that is somewhat unusual for the times:

> My dear Shawe,
> I do hope that you will allow my first communication to a non-existent lord lieutenant to be a request that one of his first acts should be to summon you to his privy council.[41]

Despite being a significant landowner and having his salary as recorder of Dublin, Frederick's correspondence reveals that, unlike his father and grandfather, he was more of a borrower than a lender. Whether this was due to providing for his six children (five sons and one daughter) or simply that he was not a good money manager it is not possible to say. A long letter dated 20 October 1858 to his financial advisors Messrs Newton and Armstrong, regarding a possible refinancing of a loan on his estate, provides a good insight into the financial entrails of the estate and how he came into it:

> Dear Sirs,
> In reply to your letter and queries with reference to the Crumlin estate, I beg to state shortly and in general terms but with substantial accuracy the following facts. The acreage of the estate is about 500 statute acres. The tenants are altogether about 30 in number. The net rental is about £1,500 per annum. I cannot tell you Griffiths valuation but I consider the lands (independently of houses and villa grounds) well worth £4 an acre for farming purposes – there is none of it bad or unprofitable. The family came into (it) by purchase of my maternal grandfather (the late Abraham Wilkinson of Bushy Park) towards the close of the last century. My mother was his only child. Mr Wilkinson died about 1804 and having made his will and left the Crumlin estate to my father for his life with remainder to my father's second son, which I am. Mr Wilkinson died possessed of considerable wealth and left no debts. My father (the late Sir Robert Shaw) enjoyed the property until 1849. In 1819 on my marriage (ratified by me on my coming of age) my father and I charged the property with £6,000 (Irish) now in question and a £400 a year incentive for my wife at the same time resetting the estate in that settlement making me tenant for life with remainder to my eldest son.

7 Kimmage Manor

I may add in the general way of observation that the property is situated within about 3 miles of Dublin on the south side. That it is in the highest state of preservation and order. That my own residence is upon it and under my constant superintendence and that although the number of tenants is altogether about 30 the bulk of the rent is paid by 10 or 12 substantial farmers – whose families have been most of them for generations in occupation of the same farms. The rest are generally persons of a very respectable class among them the clergyman and the priest of the parish and others who hold houses in the village of Crumlin and small portions of grounds for convenience that all the tenants are solvent and I may say that there are no arrears on the estate. I don't believe I owe a shilling due up to the gale day of the last month. Yours Faithfully – FS.[42]

Similarly a letter dated 16 March 1859 to the same advisors, reveals Frederick seeking a reduction of interest on a £2,000 loan from 5 per cent to 4 per cent.[43] The following day we see a further letter to Newton and Armstrong seeking a reduction in the premium he is paying on a life assurance policy on the basis that:

I was then [when he took out the policies in 1850] suffering from very severe rheumatism and hernia. I don't suffer from rheumatism now except that my figure is much bent from my former suffering and the hernia continues. My general health is excellent and my pursuits and habits are temperate and healthful … I would then beg to propose a reduction in my very heavy rate of premium. I consider that it would be reasonable and fair to charge me for the future at the ordinary rate of a man of 59.[44]

Judging by the correspondence he appears to have had very cordial relationships with his clients and was accommodating of their requests for rent deferrals or to be allowed assign lease. While flexible in his attitude, he also displays a rather emphatic nature when he perceives that a tenant or his agent is trying to take advantage of a situation, as the following correspondence from May 1852 highlights;

Dear Sir,
I beg leave to say that Mr Henry who has lately been appointed the land agent for Mr Robinson of Anniville in Co. Westmeath has discovered that a small portion of Mr Robinson's property at Crumlin was by some mistake a few years ago added to your estate occasioned I believe by the alteration of a boundary ditch … I am your humble servant – Thomas Walsh (Land Agent) 10 Middle Gardiner Street, Dublin.[45]

To which Frederick Shaw responds:

Sir,
In answer to your letter with reference to Mr Robinson's property in the parish of Crumlin I beg to say that there can be no mistake about any portion of Mr Robinson's estate being added to mine. I have myself been intimately acquainted with the ground since my boyhood and can speak with certainty of it for the last 35 years and that it is now as it was mapped by Mr Neville in 1812.[46]

Frederick Shaw's illness clearly restricted his involvement in society although when he died in July 1876 the *Irish Times* described his funeral in the following terms:

The remains of the late Recorder were yesterday morning interred in the ancient churchyard of Crumlin. The funeral was a large one and the attendance may truly be said to have included nearly all members of the Judicial Bench, the leading members of the Bar, some of the most distinguished citizens (including the Lord Mayor, the Lord Chancellor, the Lord Chief Justice).[47]

8 The grave of Sir Frederick Shaw

Within fifteen months of Sir Frederick's death, his house at Kimmage and
most of the Crumlin estate, was placed on the market on the instructions of
his second son George, Robert, his eldest son and heir to the title, having
already moved to the family seat in Bushy Park.[48]

With the passing of Frederick Shaw, third baronet, the family's importance
in the political, business and social life of Dublin and the country diminished.
Many of the family members held significant positions in the Church, military
and in commerce but none achieved the status of their Terenure forebears.

3. Politicians and community activists, 1799–1848

The late 18th-century period in Ireland was dominated by the struggle between intransigent conservative ascendancy politics and violent revolutionary movements ultimately resulting in the effective abolition of the Irish parliament and its union with Westminster. The first half of the 19th century was marked by attempts to repeal the 1800 Act of Union, to grant greater freedom and equality to Catholics and eventually the consequences of the Famine. Major occurrences such as the 1798 Rebellion, the Famine and land agitation interrupted normal political discourse and the daily lives of the citizens. Against this background this chapter hopes to contextualize the Shaw family's political credentials, to highlight the nature and scope of their involvement in mainstream local and national politics as well as their wider involvement in the community and to establish where they stood on the key issues of the day.

The family's formal involvement in politics covers a period from 1799, when Robert Shaw, the subsequent first baronet, became MP for Bannow, to 1848, when his son Frederick resigned his seat in the Westminster parliament due to ill health. While it would be exaggeration to call them political heavyweights, particularly as regards the Imperial parliament, they did make significant contributions on a range of issues and Frederick, in particular, achieved a position of considerable influence. Possibly of greater importance than their national representation was their involvement in local, and more particularly, in the much discredited municipal and county politics of Dublin.[1]

Given the success attained by the first Robert Shaw of Terenure, it is somewhat surprising that he did not participate in either local or national politics. The likelihood is however, that he would have been aware that having a political pedigree was an advantage in the Ireland of the late 18th century. In any event he seems to have availed of every opportunity to involve his son, Robert, in the affairs of the city. An example of this is the attendance of father and 20-year-old Robert junior at a meeting of the Association for the Protection of Property and the Constitution in 1795.[2] This meeting, which was formed to address the problem of unruly behavior in the capital, represented the first occasion where his attendance at an event was noted by the media of the day. There were to be many such references over the next 53 years.

The young Robert appears to have been keen to involve himself in the service of his community. At a meeting of the Rathfarnham Volunteer Corp in 1796, Lord Ely was appointed captain of the unit and Robert Shaw made cornet.[3] This association with Ely was to resurface three years later. Given Rathfarnham's proximity to the Dublin Mountains, a centre of rebel activity during the 1798 Rebellion, it is not surprising that his unit saw some active service. The Cullen papers in the National Library of Ireland describe how acting on a tip-off, a group of Rathfarnham Yeomanry under the command of Captain Robert Shaw and Captain George La Touche raided William Kearney's Inn near Bohernabreena on the night of 27 July 1798 and gave chase to a group of United Irishmen who included Robert Emmet. Shaw was fortunate to have avoided injury or even death when he was dissuaded by a Mrs Kearney from accessing an attic where the United Irishmen were hiding.[4] Shaw remained involved in various forms of militia for the rest of his life and was often referred to as Colonel Shaw in newspaper articles in later years as a result of his being appointed colonel of the Royal Dublin Militia in 1821.[5]

It was through his association with Lord Ely that in 1799 Robert Shaw first entered national politics. Ely, through the family's estates, controlled a number of electoral boroughs. One of these was Bannow, Co. Wexford and it was for this constituency that Robert became an MP in the Irish Parliament in March 1799. Against the expectations of his patron, Shaw was an anti-Unionist and Ely who was pro-Union forced him to forfeit his seat by means of acceptance of an escheatorship (Munster) which was a mechanism that circumvented the illegality of a serving MP resigning. However, Shaw was soon back in the parliamentary fold when he purchased a seat for St Johnstown in Co. Longford from the earl of Granard in February 1800. This type of parliamentary manoeuvering was not uncommon in the final years of the College Green parliament. Geoghegan maintains that in 1800, a year when there was no election, of 33 boroughs representing 66 seats, 106 different people were returned for parliament within a space of just six months, as the authorities sought to ensure a majority for the Union bill that was about to be put before the house.[6] Amid allegations of bribery, threats and patronage a majority for the bill was achieved and was passed by 158 to 115 receiving royal assent on 1 August 1800.[7] Shaw was one of those who voted against it and was to remain an advocate of Repeal for the rest of his political life.

Following the Union, the Irish representation in Westminster was 100 MPs. The initial representation was chosen from the outgoing 300 Irish parliament members. As an MP representing a borough rather than a county or city, Shaw was not automatically entitled to a seat and along with 234 others was entered into a draw to fill 34 places. He did not obtain a seat under the ballot system and remained outside of national representative politics for four years until March 1804 when he was elected MP for Dublin City in a by election, following the resignation of John Claudius Beresford.[8] From 1804 to 1826 Shaw successfully fought five further election campaigns for Dublin City. In all cases he was joined in parliament by Henry Grattan.

In the days before 'whip based' party politics, politicians operated in a rather looser arrangement than exists today. In this context Shaw, and indeed his son Frederick, were affiliated to the Tory grouping whose leaders in the Imperial parliament included the likes of Pitt, Peel, Lord Liverpool and Arthur Wellesley, better known as the duke of Wellington. Until the election of O'Connell in 1828 and the advent of the Repeal Party, politics in Dublin was contested between those affiliated to the Tories and those associated with the Whigs (Liberals) such as Grattan.

Politics in the first half of the 19th century could hardly be regarded as either representative or democratic. It was unrepresentative in that few of the majority Catholic population were entitled to vote, women were totally excluded and there were significant property ownership qualifications required: for instance, up until the first quarter of the 19th century only those men who held freehold property with a valuation of 40s. could vote. In effect, voting was restricted to Protestant property owning men, who were approached by the relevant candidates through their various guild and trade associations. An indication of how confined the electorate was can be gleaned from the results of the 1806 election for Dublin City. The total votes cast were 4,835 at a time when the population of the city was almost 200,000. Henry Grattan (1,675) and Robert Shaw (1,638) took the two seats from John La Touche (1,522).[9]

To have any chance of being elected, candidates had to seek the support of an eclectic range of craft and trade guilds. Papers at election times carried advertisements from groups such as the corporation of cooks, the guild of carpenters, corporation of weavers, supporting one candidate or another. For instance:

Corporation of sheermen and dyers
At a meeting of the above Corporation, the 13 March, 1804, ... the following resolutions were agreed to: −
Resolved that our worthy fellow citizen, Robert Shaw, Esq. is a proper person to be candidate to represent this city in Parliament, in the room of our worthy and much respected fellow citizen J.C. Beresford, Esq. who has resigned. Resolved that this Corporation will support Mr. Shaw with their votes and interest upon the ensuing election, without expense to him on our account. Resolved that the Master, Wardens and Numbers be a committee to wait on Mr Shaw with the foregoing resolutions, and that the same, together with his answer be published in the public newspapers.[10]

Campaigns were fought out in the meeting rooms of the various guilds and corporations until the arrival of O'Connell in the 1820s, when they moved to the streets. Lobbying of members of the guilds was popular with candidates seeking endorsements from various groups e.g.

General election – city of Dublin
To the gentlemen, clergy, freemen, and freeholders of the city of Dublin
A dissolution of Parliament having taken place. I beg leave again to offer myself to your consideration and to solicit the honour of your support to replace me in the high and elevated situation of one of your representatives ... Shall I again be fortunate as to become the object of your choice, it shall be the study of my life, as it has heretofore been, to show my gratitude by an unceasing anxiety to promote, by every means in my power, the welfare and prosperity of the country at large and more particularly that of the City of Dublin. RS[11]

For 19th-century politicians the focus was on promoting the sectional interests of local groups in parliament. Thus we see in 1809 a petition to Shaw to represent the interest of the inhabitants of the barony of Rathdown to oppose a proposed Bill to erect turnpikes in the barony.[12] He also supported the brewers in their resolution to lower the duty on beer.[13] Shaw was not averse to letting it be known to the widest possible audience of his support for popular causes, as evidenced by an advertisement placed in the daily papers declaring his support for the corporation of carpenters, in fighting an increase of 50 per cent in window light tax:

To the Corporation of carpenters
Gentlemen, In reply to your resolutions, I beg to assure you, I shall be happy to give my support to any measures most likely to promote the object of your wishes and the general prosperity of the country.[14]

In fairness to politicians it would appear from vehement correspondence appearing on the letter pages of newspapers that it was unwise to ignore the petitions of electors as the following extract illustrates:

To Robert Shaw, Esq. M.P. for Dublin,
Sir, I am one of those who voted for you at the last election for our city, upon principle, and from conviction that you were a man who honestly, faithfully, fearlessly and impartially do your duty. I shall now put you to the test, and if you shrink from, or equivocate in the discharge of the obligations which you have solemnly undertaken, I frankly tell you, that, when a general election comes, you will meet with the most active opposition from one of your most useful friends.
Yours a Citizen[15]

While Shaw's main contributions in parliament concerned matters relating to Dublin, he also on occasion addressed issues such as repeal of the Union and Catholic emancipation. His speeches contain little innovative or interesting thinking and convey little of his political philosophies or insight into his true character. One change that does appear to have taken place in his political thinking is in relation to his position on relief for Catholics. While not a member of the 'Ultra Protestant movement' whose members included the likes of John Giffard and Dr Patrick Duigenan, he was nonetheless a staunch supporter of the Established Church.[16] In 1805 he was spokesman for the 'Protestant interests against Catholic claims' on Dublin Corporation and in 1808, he like his son would do thirty-eight years later, vehemently opposed the increasing of grant aid to St Patrick's College, Maynooth. After 1812 he appears to have softened his attitude and supported improving the rights of Roman Catholics.[17] Evidence of this can be seen in the address of a delegation of Catholics from Thomastown in Co. Kilkenny in 1813:

> Sir, We the Roman Catholics of Thomastown, beg to embrace this opportunity of congratulating you on your arrival amongst us … We feel deeply impressed with sentiments of gratitude for the kindness evinced to us by your truly honourable father, who, among other favours, made a present of a valuable piece of ground to erect a chapel on: and that at a period when bigotry was encouraged and liberality prescribed. Liberal as that donation has been, its value is now greatly enhanced by the additional ground you have granted us, for the further convenience of parishioners.[18]

The national political career of Robert Shaw, first baronet, while spanning over twenty-two years did not secure for him high office. By contrast his career in the local politics of both the city and county of Dublin saw him rise to the most senior posts in both areas.

A parliamentary report in 1835 summed up the situation with regard to local government in Ireland in the early 19th century, when it concluded that the Irish corporations had long ceased to pay any attention to the interests or welfare of the inhabitants of Irish cities or towns, but devoted their energies to protecting the position of a narrow politically sectarian class. The report stated that ' aggravated by their being considered inimical, on the ground of sectarian feelings, to a great majority of the resident population, and they become instrumental to the continuance of the unhappy dissentions which it has so long been the policy of the legislature to allay.'[19] In essence therefore the government saw local bodies, like Dublin Corporation, as promoting unrest and mistrust of the administration and therefore in need of overhaul.

In keeping with his prominent business profile and his desire to be involved in political life, Robert Shaw served on Dublin Corporation from the late 1790s. He was high sheriff of Dublin in 1797 but resigned this post 'on payment of a fine of £300' for a reason unknown to the author but is listed as a 'sheriffs peer' in 1799. By 1809 he was listed as one of twenty-four aldermen thus entitling him to life membership of the Corporation. In 1815 at the age of 41 he was lord mayor of Dublin.[20]

Dublin Corporation around the time that Robert Shaw was lord mayor (1815/16) was a largely upper-middle-class Protestant, unionist body. The metamorphosis to a Catholic and Repeal-based institution was yet to occur. As such it was largely unrepresentative of the vast majority of the city's population. Unlike the current city council it was not an elected body in terms of the citizens electing members. It consisted of a lord mayor, 24 aldermen who were entitled to seats in the assembly for life, and 144 common council men (commoners), made up of 48 sheriffs peers and 96 representatives from the various merchant and trade guilds in the city. All of these were drawn from a base of approximately 4,000 hereditary freemen.[21] As such, its members were drawn from the most affluent sectors of society with little affiliation with general population.

As the following address from 1815 by Alderman John Cash indicates, the corporation was almost sycophantic in their loyalty to the monarchy:

> The peace, celebration of the centenary of the accession of the illustrious House of Hanover, and the anniversary of the birth of his royal highness the Prince Regent formed a brilliant epoch. The rejoicings on this occasion within my jurisdiction were spontaneous, cordial and universal, and I had the happiness to find that the conduct of the inhabitants during the three days festival was distinguished by propriety, regularity and order, as much as by a spirit of loyalty.[22]

Similarly the occasion of the bombardment of Algiers by the British navy and the subsequent freeing of 3,000 European slaves elicited the following effusive tribute that was unanimously adopted by the members:

> We, his majesty's most faithful and loyal subjects … whose hearts are filled with sincere joy at the glorious success of his majesty's arms, beg leave to congratulate your Royal Highness upon your splendid achievement … When we consider the spirit which animated your Royal Highness to this great act, the wisdom of your councils, the exertions of your ministers, the skill of your forces, and those of your illustrious ally (king of Belgium), but above all the celebrity with which the thunder of Britain was turned against the enemy of our faith. We are lost in admiration and can only give you humble and grateful thanks to the great Creator and governor of the universe for having blessed your efforts with such great signal success.[23]

While originally responsible for all aspects of the city's affairs these were eventually allotted to other administrative bodies such as the Board of Works.

As a consequence of this stripping away of responsibilities, the corporation more or less became a 'talking shop' with few real powers. Such was its alienation from the running of the city that the aforementioned 1835 enquiry could say that it was 'almost totally disconnected from the administration of funds, and relieved from the performance of the trusts'.[24] Despite this, there does not appear to have been any unwillingness by the upper echelons of Dublin society to participate in its work. Names such as Arthur Guinness, Nathaniel Hone, John Claudius Beresford, William Archer and Frederick Darley all leading business figures in the community, were on the corporation at different times, so it clearly had advantages in terms of social status, influence on decisions or as a stepping stone for greater political ambitions. Certainly Daniel O'Connell used his tenure on the council to further his own political ends and career.

A review of the decisions taken by the corporation during the period when Robert Shaw was lord mayor provides an interesting insight into its powers and the way they impacted on society. For instance among the matters dealt with by the city assembly in April 1815 included the following:

1. The granting of a petition of Michael Clarke for renewal of a lease on a premises in Chatham Street.
2. That the Commission for wide streets be asked to make considerable improvements Essex Street.
3. Seeking advice from the recorder on terminating tenancies of tenants where the lives of the leases have expired.
4. Matters concerning the regulation of wholesale markets in the city.
5. Appointment of Frederick Bournes as gaoler of Newgate Prison – Mr Bournes to provide an indemnity to the corporation from all escapes.
6. Granting of the freedom of the city to the earls of Mayo, Howth and Arthur Brooke.
7. Heard petitions from various parties re their seeking appointment or retention of various positions e.g. engineer of the pipe water works, basin keeper Blessington Street (salary £1 per week) etc.
8. Appointment of various civic positions such as sergeant of the mace, sword bearers, constable, master of the city works.
9. Hearing petitions and making grants such as 'Mary Gregg, widow, praying for aid; whereupon it was ordered, that the petitioner be paid the sum of £25, for the reasons in her petition mentioned.
10. Approving of certain municipal contracts for trades.[25]

It is also interesting to note that while members of the corporation, like MPs at the time, were unpaid there were certain financial rewards availed of by members. Thus, in 1816 following his year as lord mayor, we see Robert Shaw petitioning the Assembly as follows:

That your petitioner has served the office of chief magistrate for the last year, he trusts with becoming dignity and in such manner as to meet with your approbation of his fellow citizens. That by act of the Easter assembly 1813, one thousand pounds part of the allowance for succeeding chief magistrates, is to be petitioned for at the expiration of their respective mayoralties. May it please your lordship and honours to pay your petitioner the sum of £1,000. Whereupon as the minutes record, the treasurer was ordered to pay the said amount.[26]

While Frederick Shaw never sat on the Dublin City Assembly, his opposition to the Irish municipal corporations bill, as it passed through parliament in 1835, makes clear his attitude to attempts to make such bodies more representative:

While he would never set his face against real improvement, come from what quarter it might, he certainly would not be a consenting party to place the municipal authorities and local jurisdiction throughout Ireland in the hands of those whose avowed object was to subvert the Established Church in that country, and whose scarcely concealed motive was to separate its institutions from Great Britain.[27]

If Dublin Corporation was a maligned institution in the early part of the 19th century, its county equivalent, the Grand Jury was even more so. Even less representative than the corporation, the members were chosen by the high sheriff from the leading landowners of the relevant county. The selection process meant that juries were usually made up of friends and associates of the high sheriff and they became self-perpetuating bodies. The system was the subject of much criticism and was the subject of many parliamentary investigations.[28] While discredited, they were very powerful and influential in administering the affairs of counties in terms of road and bridge building, provision of medical facilities, and the erection and running of prisons among other functions.

Robert Shaw qualified for membership of the Co. Dublin Grand Jury by reason of the family estates in Terenure and Crumlin. He was made high sheriff of County Dublin in 1806 and served as a grand juror for many years thereafter. The Co. Dublin Grand Jury in the first quarter of the 19th century contained many of the most prominent Dublin families such as the Talbots, the Domvilles, Vershoyles, Hamiltons, Foots, and of course Shaws.

While perhaps justifiably open to criticism, the author's review of the Dublin Grand Jury minutes for the 1818/19 period, show it to operate on a business like and professional basis. For instance, over the two-year-period reviewed, the jurors met on four occasions in November and February each year and each session lasted for between five and nine days. The minutes record almost full attendance at all sessions.

There was little evidence of the jingoistic type addresses to the monarchy which were characteristic of the Dublin City Assembly and the minutes convey a business-like attitude to dealing with the matters before it. By way of illustration, the following matters came before the committee during the period for which the minutes were reviewed:

1. Decision that the county Grand Jury would meet with the City Assembly on Monday 23 November 1818, for the purpose of discussing a parliamentary bill regarding the Wide Street Commissioners.
2. Decision to meet the Grand Jury of Wicklow for the purposes of discussing the line for an intended new mail coach road between Dublin and Waterford in the Co. of Dublin near Brittas. Shaw, Foot, Finlay et al. be appointed to meet the Wicklow Grand Jury.
3. Report on the committee on the gaol of Kilmainham received. The report contains very detailed comparisons for the earnings of convicts in UK prisons. A recommendation that those in gaol for non-payment of debts to be removed immediately to the Four Courts, Marshalsea gaol.
4. Decision to withhold certain funds from various dispensaries.
5. Approval for repairs to be made to the Fox and Geese road.
6. A decision to form a sub-committee of Shaw, Church, Needham, Finlay, Arabin and Bourne to apply for an act of parliament to establish a turnpike road from Dolphin's Barn to Clane.[29]

The Grand Juries were seen as unrepresentative, lacking in transparency and corrupt. As a senior juror of long standing, Robert Shaw did little to change this image. None of his sons became grand jurors but his grandson, also Robert, did serve as high sheriff for Co. Dublin in 1848 and for many years thereafter as juror.

Frederick Shaw's political career began in 1830. Given his holding of various senior administrative positions such as recorder for Dundalk (1826–8), recorder for Dublin (1828–76), secretary to the master of the rolls (1827), and attorney general (1834), he did not engage in electoral politics, until he succeeded to his father's old seat in Dublin city in the 1830 general election. Ironically he defeated the son of his father's old electoral sparring partner, Henry Grattan in that election.[30] Unfortunately for Shaw, the Whig Government of Earl Grey was forced to call a general election within ten months on the issue of electoral reform and Shaw lost out to the Whig candidates Robert Harty and Louis Perrin. However, following a petition, the two successful candidates were unseated and Shaw was awarded one of the seats. Reading correctly the changed political landscape in Dublin, which saw the election of two Repeal candidates (Daniel O'Connell and Edward Southwell Ruthven) in the General election of 1832, Shaw switched to the more conservative and less competitive constituency of Dublin University, where he successfully won seats in the general elections of 1832, 1835, 1837, 1841 and 1847.

Frederick Shaw was a more active parliamentarian than his father. He spoke on a variety of topics ranging from atmospheric railways to the sale of the Hafod estate in Wales, and was chairman of a number of select committees. His most acclaimed contribution came in his defence of Sir William Cusack Smith, when he managed to have a resolution rescinded which had been proposed by Daniel O'Connell to establish a select committee 'to inquire into the conduct of Baron Smith in respect of his neglect of duty as a judge, and the introduction of political topics in his charges to grand juries'. However, it was his contributions concerning funding for St Patrick's College Maynooth and those relating to the repeal of the Corn Laws and the extension of the Poor Law Relief schemes during the famine of 1845–7 that provide the greatest insight into his political thinking. With a reputation for being an excellent debater, he became the unofficial leader of the Irish Conservative MPs at Westminster. He was not an extreme Tory and his support for Catholic emancipation prior to his election isolated him somewhat from the more extreme elements of the Tory movement in Ireland, such as his brother-in-law, the earl of Roden, who was the leader of the Irish Tories in the Lords. As discussed in an earlier chapter when Peel came to power in 1834, Shaw was offered the post of lord lieutenant of Ireland, but he turned it down in favour of a seat on the Irish Privy Council.[31] He was regarded as a close confidant and advisor to Lord Haddington, whom Peel had appointed lord lieutenant when Shaw refused, and Haddington's short reign of just four months, was known as the 'Shaw viceroyalty' by his political opponents.[32]

After the Reform Act of 1832, Daniel O'Connell had hopes that Shaw would stand as a Conservative repeal candidate, but this did not turn out to be the case and probably was responsible for his change to the Dublin University constituency for the election of that year. In a letter to William Scott, the high sheriff of Dublin dated 25 October 1832, O'Connell states with regard to Shaw 'I did offer the Recorder to stand for Dublin along with him if he thought that conjunction would facilitate his return upon the explicit Repeal pledge – the open and avowed basis of our co-operation to be Repeal and nothing but Repeal ... I need not add that he would not pledge himself to Repeal, and so the matter finally ended.'[33] Henceforth Shaw and O'Connell would be rivals. O'Connell's letter to his friend P.V. Fitzpatrick, dated 18 July 1835, on the subject of the Municipal corporations bill indicates how he viewed Shaw: 'Peel knows that this country cannot be governed by the Tories. Let Shaw be as bombastic as he pleases, I have a strong feeling that the Orange Party are down forever.'[34]

Shaw's position on repeal of the Union is somewhat surprising since his father voted against the original legislation and remained a 'repealer' all his life. No material was discovered in the course of this study that provided insight into why father and son had opposing views.

In a speech relating to the funding of St Patrick's College Maynooth in 1845, Shaw showed his political skill by using the opportunity afforded to counteract arguments from Catholic lobby groups for representation on the governing body of Dublin University. His response provides insight into the views of Protestants into the increasing pressure from Catholics to gain greater say in a whole host of areas that they were previously excluded from:

> The University of Dublin was open equally to Roman Catholics as to Protestants for all purposes of education and that, not only in theory, but practically, the Roman Catholic gentry enjoyed the full benefit of its honours and degrees … It is most unreasonable for Roman Catholics to clamour for admission to the governing body of an establishment which was essentially Protestant and essentially connected with the Established Church.[35]

With the benefit of hindsight, Shaw's contributions to motions relating to various forms of Famine relief are likely to remain his least impressive political legacy. He did, eventually and rather reluctantly support Peel in repealing certain aspects of the Corn Laws in 1846. From his contributions, which are worth quoting at some length, we see that despite the mounting evidence of horrific human suffering, he seemed unable or unwilling to see the problem for what it was, namely, a tragedy of immense proportions. He saw the famine of 1845–8 as resulting from a series of bad harvests all-too-familiar in Ireland and a situation that was exploited by groups seeking to undermine the regime, or to bring about a change in the economic principle of *laissez faire*, which he, as a conservative, held dear. Hansard's record of his speech, in response to a motion by John O'Connell MP, in February 1846, relating to the Drainage Ireland bill illustrates the point;

> Mr Shaw urged upon government the great importance of resisting, from the first, every attempt to introduce outdoor relief, or anything in the nature of a labour rate, in connection with Poor Law in Ireland. The law itself, after having encountered great difficulty and opposition, was only beginning fairly to operate in that country. The workhouses were not yet nearly full, not withstanding the emergency to which the Rt. Hon gentleman had alluded; but should they become full, and even as the case stood at present, the burden of the poor rate was as heavy as those subject to it could well bear. As the emergency of the potato failure in Ireland had been referred to, he could no further go into the question at present than to say that, while he deplored the occurrence of any

failure, and desired every means to be taken to alleviate such distress as
it might occasion, still he was bound to say, that he considered the extent
of the failure had been greatly exaggerated.[36]

In an address to the House later in February 1846, he made the claim that
the situation is being deliberately exploited and that government inspectors
had been 'imposed upon':

> But as the question of the potato failure in Ireland had become so
> prominent in the debates of the House and so paramount in influencing
> the measures of the Government, he thought it right to inform the
> house of the real facts of the case, as he believed them to be, without
> adding to or taking from them. The statement of the honourable and
> learned gentleman must be borne in mind, that there was scarcely a
> season in Ireland, especially towards its close, that there was not scarcity
> and consequent distress in many parts of the country. The poor law
> commissioners ... reported that for some portions of the year, upwards
> of two million of the population were without the means of procuring
> food, and in a state of destitution. That there would be an aggravation
> of the usual periodical distress during the ensuing season, he grieved to
> say he could not doubt; but still he was bound to add, that he considered
> very exaggerated statements had been put forth, and undue alarm
> excited on the subject.[37]

He went on to question why Dr Playfair and Mr Lindley had concluded
that a serious situation existed in that half of the potato crop had failed, and
he said 'that no practical man in Ireland who did not believe that they had
been imposed upon.' He added that he had spoken with friends in Cork,
Tipperary, Kilkenny, Carlow, Wicklow, Co. Dublin, Donegal, Fermanagh,
Tyrone, Down and Mayo and from this he believed that there was 'an average
crop while in some areas there would be a considerable deficiency – an
admission quite sufficient to justify every precaution the Government could
take against even the possible calamity of a partial famine.'[38]
    It is difficult to understand why Shaw failed to see the serious extent of
this particular famine given that it was having a serious affect on his own
district. In fact, he need not have gone further than to speak to his own son,
Robert, who as chairman of the local Rathmines Relief Committee, was
dealing with the impact of famine in the area as we see in letters he was
sending to MPs and various Government officials for financial aid to assist the
destitute in Harolds Cross and Milltown. In January 1847 we see him writing
to Henry Labouchere:

As chairman of the Rathmines Relief Committee I beg to address you for the purpose of ascertaining whether Her Majesty's Government will grant a sum of money in aid of the funds collected by private subscriptions for the relief of the poor. The district for which the committee has been appointed is extensive and comprises two very poor and populous localities – Milltown and Harold's Cross. These contain a large number both of labouring and destitute poor … To enable them to purchase food at something approaching a reasonable price the committee have opened a poor shop where meal and rice are sold on tickets at a small reduction under cost price … The quantity sold to each per week is proportionate to the number in (the) family. By this means upwards of 300 families are relieved. The Committee have also opened a Soup Shop similar to those already established in the metropolis where tickets are sold to the poor who are able to purchase them. They are thus provided with a cheap and nutritious food. The committee have as yet only been able to collect £240. This fund will soon be exhausted.[39]

In addition to the setting up of meal shops and soup kitchens in Rathmines, centres to alleviate the widespread distress were also established in neighbouring villages such as Tallaght and Clondalkin. How Frederick Shaw could have failed to see the unprecedented situation that existed on his own doorstep is hard to understand. As his speeches in the House highlight, he appears to have been influenced by the writings of various political economists such as Adam Smith, Malthus and Ricardo.[40] His speeches indicate that he was a proponent of the non-interventionist teachings expounded by Smith and Ricardo rather than the more interventionist approach espoused by Malthus, to the economic management of the economy. As history has shown us over the centuries, strict adherence to rigid doctrines particularly at inflexion points can give rise to seriously erroneous judgments.

While hindsight affords us an opportunity to realize the error in Shaw's thinking, at the time he most certainly was not alone in his views. In the general election of August 1847, in which Shaw was again returned for Dublin University, the Famine was not the dominant electoral issue and in some constituencies did not even feature.[41] The key issues in this election were Repeal and extensions to civil and political liberties. Whether the lack of focus had to do with an 'information deficit', a sense that the worst was over or the fact that those who suffered most, namely the poor, were electorally irrelevant is unclear. What is clear is that, in the face of the greatest tragedy to hit Ireland, there was no sense of urgency or cohesion among the 105 Irish MPs in Westminster to address the catastrophe. In that sense Frederick Shaw was not in any way unique in his approach to the problem.

Frederick Shaw stood for and won a seat in the 1847 general election. Within a year he had resigned, using the mechanism known as the 'Steward of the Chiltern Hundreds' to vacate his seat. The stated reason for his resignation was ill health brought about by severe rheumatism. While undoubtedly afflicted by the ailment, one wonders if isolation from his more religiously right-wing Tory colleagues, or from those who saw his voting with Peel in the Repeal of the Corn Laws motion, as a betrayal of the *laissez faire* philosophy that dominated Conservative party thinking at the time, were contributory factors to his decision to resign his seat.

His departure from political life at the age of 49 brought to an end the family's fifty-year involvement in national and local politics. It also represented the point where the Shaws, apart from literary relative George Bernard Shaw (1856–1950), would cease to be prominent in Irish public life and would all but disappear in 20th-century, independent Ireland.

Conclusion

A brief report which appeared in the *Irish Times* in March 1953 epitomized the changes that occurred in Irish society over the previous 167 years, better than many of the volumes that have been written about the history of the period. The paper reported:

> Dublin Corporation last night approved the decision of the Finance and General Purposes Committee to sell Bushy Park House, Terenure and about 20 acres of the grounds for £8,000 as a site for a Catholic girls' secondary school … The Committee's report stated that the Most Rev. Dr McQuaid, Archbishop of Dublin, had requested that portion of the estate be made available for the school.[1]

There are many ironies in the situation described. The first was that Bushy Park House, for long a bastion of Protestantism, was now in the ownership of an order of Catholic nuns, especially when one considers that the family's other house, Kimmage Manor, had already passed into the ownership of the Holy Ghost Fathers for use as a seminary for training priests. The second irony was that it was Dublin Corporation that was selling the property at the instigation of the Catholic archbishop of Dublin. This, the same Corporation that Robert Shaw had headed as lord mayor, and which was then so tightly controlled by the Protestant ruling classes, was now susceptible to the influence of the Catholic hierarchy. One can only imagine the number of rotations many of the family members did in their graves at this turn of events.

In many ways the above article provides a clue as to why the Shaws have all but been forgotten. The world which they inhabited had changed so utterly that the family simply ceased to have any relevance in the fledgling republic, where people were keen to cast off the memories of the past. Unlike the rural landed estates where landlords, albeit ever decreasingly, continued to have some degree of impact on local economies, the merchant estates had little or no effect and hence ceased to be relevant to the local communities. While the family enjoyed great power and influence in their day, it is questionable if they ever fully integrated with their neighbours or the wider Terenure and Crumlin communities. This study has not found any evidence of strong local links or of a major contribution in terms of providing buildings or monuments to the locality.

The story of the Shaw family during the period 1786 to 1876 draws together numerous themes, many of which have received little attention in the historical chronicles of the time. Among the most salient are the creation, management and the disbursal of wealth amongst the family members. The story of the Shaws shows how the practice of primogeniture, despite its apparent unfairness to the modern eye, was used as a means of keeping family wealth intact through the generations. Their story also epitomizes how wealth can be dissipated as subsequent generations lost the entrepreneurial drive and ambition shown by their earlier forefathers who had exemplified the 'Protestant work ethic'.

Moreover, the history of the Shaw family reveals the emergence of an entrepreneurial mercantile class, and their taking of power, both political and economic from the landed aristocracy. This group, which included the Guinnesses, La Touches and Shaws, dominated Dublin political and commercial life for most of the period. With the notable exception of the Guinness family none of their empires or influence survived into the 20th century. In addition, the study illustrates the importance of social networking from the perspective of politics, social life and business. A recurring theme is the regularity with which the same small group of names appear in local government bodies, business ventures and charitable and social activities. The Dublin of the period was a small place, where being part of the ruling Protestant elite, was essential for progression in career, business and politics. The Shaws were adroit at creating and managing these networks as their business dealings and marriage arrangements highlight. The family's business and personal financial dealings provide insight into how business was conducted in the period. The recurring economic cycle of boom and bust showed Ireland's dependence on agriculture and is in contrast to the emerging industrial economies of Britain, Europe and North America. The period saw rapid change in banking practices from the emergence of formalized private banks to the establishment of their joint stock equivalents, which laid the foundation of modern Ireland's banking infrastructure.

Furthermore, a crucial aspect of the background to the family story is the growing demand from Catholics for greater civil and personal liberties. The Shaw family epitomized in many respects the attitude of the members of the Established Church to these threats. Their response, which elsewhere saw a growth in extremism such as the formation of the Orange Order and the Ultra-Protestant movements and the emergence of a siege mentality so typical of such situations, was reflected in their contribution to political debate. By extension a key theme that emerges is how narrow and unrepresentative national and local politics were. The politics of the day were unashamedly based on sectional interests such as the landlords that dominated the grand jury system or the craft and trade guilds and corporations that controlled the Dublin City Assembly. In keeping with many of their contemporaries the

Shaws appeared to subscribe to the notion that the rule of the enlightened was superior to the tyranny of the majority. In this connection, a significant feature that marked the period was the concept of *noblese oblige*. The willingness of the middle classes to engage so extensively in charitable and public works contributed significantly to ameliorating the suffering of those less fortunate. This approach is in stark contrast to the doctrine of *laissez faire* that epitomized most political thinking of the time and resulted in huge social inequalities and unfairness.

While the sale of the family's estate in the early 1950s represented their formal departure from the Terenure area, the reality was that their decline from prominence had started one hundred years earlier with the death of Sir Robert Shaw, the first baronet in 1849. He along with his father was responsible for building the family fortune which was the basis of their power and prominence. While a number of their descendants were to make a mark on life none had the energy or entrepreneurial drive exhibited by the first two Roberts.

The decline of a family, such as the Shaws, can be put down to many historical and social influences but in the end it was their failure to adapt to the changing environment that was Ireland in the late 19th and early 20th century. Maybe they would have done well to apply the wisdom of their most famous family member, George Bernard Shaw, when he said 'The reasonable man adapts himself to the world; the unreasonable one persists in trying to adapt the world to himself. Therefore all progress depends on the unreasonable man.' Maybe they were just too reasonable.

Appendices

APPENDIX I: SHAW FAMILY TREE

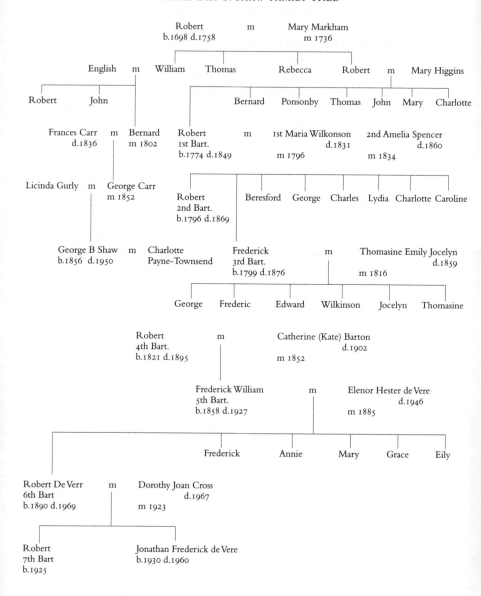

Robert b.1698 d.1758　m　Mary Markham m 1736

English　m　William　Thomas　　Rebecca　Robert　m　Mary Higgins

Robert　John

Bernard　Ponsonby　Thomas　John　Mary　Charlotte

Frances Carr d.1836　m　Bernard m 1802

Robert 1st Bart. b.1774 d.1849　m　1st Maria Wilkonson d.1831 m 1796　　2nd Amelia Spencer d.1860 m 1834

Licinda Gurly　m　George Carr m 1852

Robert 2nd Bart. b.1796 d.1869　Beresford　George　Charles　Lydia　Charlotte　Caroline

George B Shaw b.1856 d.1950　m　Charlotte Payne-Townsend

Frederick 3rd Bart. b.1799 d.1876　m　Thomasine Emily Jocelyn d.1859 m 1816

George　Frederic　Edward　Wilkinson　Jocelyn　Thomasine

Robert 4th Bart. b.1821 d.1895　m　Catherine (Kate) Barton d.1902 m 1852

Frederick William 5th Bart. b.1858 d.1927　m　Elenor Hester de Vere d.1946 m 1885

Frederick　Annie　Mary　Grace　Eily

Robert De Verr 6th Bart b.1890 d.1969　m　Dorothy Joan Cross d.1967 m 1923

Robert 7th Bart b.1925　　Jonathan Frederick de Vere b.1930 d.1960

APPENDIX 2: TERENURE ESTATE RENTS
Terenure Estate rents 1869 – Rent Ledger – MS 9450 – NLI

Tenant	Annual Rent			
Rev Eugene Cullen	£261	1s.	6d.	Including income tax '@ 5d. in £ – poor Rate @ 1/6 in £
William O'Brien Smith	£12	18s.	4d.	
Mrs Vincent	£64	7s.	10d.	
C R Whitton	£114	16s.	2d.	Poor rate 1/6, 1/4, 2/–, 2/10
Edward Wright	£104	10s.		
Thomas Moyers	£83	16s.	10d.	
James Daly	£20			
Rev James Elliott	£55	7s.	8d.	
John R Mallins	£285	6s.	6d.	No increases over 1869–74
Samuel Stephens	£53	8s.	4d.	
James Hartley	£65	2s.	4d.	
reps of the late Mrs Darley	£145	13s.	8d.	
John Flynn	£31	10s.		
John O'Bonsall	£21	9s.	6d.	
William Franklin	£53	13s.		
Edward Nolan – rep of J Taylor decd	£15			
Rev John Hall	£15			
Joseph Traynor	£24			
Edward Rothwell	£22			
John Lennon	£10	10s.		
David Rogerson	£85	17s.	10d.	
Nicholas Flood	£40			
Reps of Patrick Regan	£24			
Peter Tracy	£10			
William Nolan	£13	16s.	10d.	
J E Scott	£39	15s.		
Mrs Hayes	£5	5s.		
William Manley	£10			
Robert Kerr Dispensary	£10			
Richard Kellett	£125			
John Manley	£20			
James Clarke	£10			
James Neill	£10			
R W O'Callaghan	£40			
reps John Keefe	£140			
John Bonds	£40			
James Kavanagh	£6			
Patrick Levy	£6			
Thomas Jordan	£17			River Strand Bushy Park
Gerald Osbrey	£85	0s.	10d.	
E J Duilton	£89	1s.		
William James Connor	£22			
Miss Shaw	£5			
Thomas Green	£250			house and farm
Mr Peakin	£260			Part of the demense of BP plus 10 acres of grazing land
Mr Gills / M Kavanagh	£5			
Total annual rent	£2,936	18s.	2d.	

Notes

ABBREVIATIONS

AIB   Allied Irish Bank Group
BL   British Library
DCA   Dublin City Archives
DCL   Dublin City Library
FS   Frederick Shaw
HC   House of Commons
MP   Member of Parliament
NAI   National Archives of Ireland
NLI   National Library of Ireland
RDS   Royal Dublin Society
RS   Robert Shaw

INTRODUCTION

1   *Burke's peerage & baronetage* (London, 1999, 106th edition), ii, pp 2592–3.
2   *Walker's Hibernian Magazine,* obituary of Robert Shaw, July 1796.
3   Kenneth Milne, *History of the Royal Bank of Ireland* (Dublin, 1964).

1 MERCHANTS AND BANKERS

1   *Walker's Hibernian Magazine,* July 1796.
2   L.M. Cullen, *An economic history of Ireland since 1660* (London, 1972), p. 83.
3   Peter Somerville Large, *Dublin – the fair city* (London, 1996), p. 152.
4   Thomas and Valerie Pakenham, *Dublin – a traveller's companion* (London, 1988), p. 58.
5   Cullen, *Economic history of Ireland,* p. 95.
6   *Wilson's Directory,* 1786.
7   J.T. Gilbert, *A history of the city of Dublin* (3 vols Dublin, 1978), iii, p. 364.
8   Sundry transactions of Shaw family finances 1784–93 (NLI, MS 5610).

9   F.G. Hall, *The Bank of Ireland 1783–1946* (Dublin, 1949), p. 508.
10   P.H. Gulliver and M. Silverman, *Merchants and shop-keepers, an historical anthropology of an Irish market town, 1200–1991* (London, 1995), p. 93.
11   Ledger of Robert Shaw & son, merchants and bill holders, 1785–90 (NLI, MS 5681).
12   Letter book of Robert Shaw & son, merchants and bill holders, 1793–7 (NLI, MS 5678).
13   NLI, MS 5678.
14   NLI, MS 5681.
15   NLI, MS 5681.
16   NLI, MS 5678.
17   Rowena Dudley, *The Irish lottery, 1780–1801* (Dublin, 2005), p. 27.
18   Ibid., pp 93–4.
19   Ibid., p. 95.
20   Ibid., p. 96.
21   NLI, MS 5681.
22   NLI, MS 5681.
23   *Freeman's Journal,* 28 Feb. 1810.
24   Letter book of Robert Shaw & Son, 29 July 1796–14 October 1797 (NLI, MS 5680).
25   Hall, *Bank of Ireland,* p. 4.

26 E. Powell, *The evolution of the money market* (1385–1915) (1915: rpt, Dublin, 1964), p. 23.
27 Hall, *Bank of Ireland*, p. 119.
28 NLI, MS 5681.
29 Milne, *Royal Bank*, p. 9.
30 NLI, MS 5681.
31 Milne, *Royal Bank*, p. 16.
32 *Freeman's Journal*, 10 Jan. 1812
33 Hall, *Bank of Ireland*, p. 131.
34 Michael Mc Ginley, *The La Touche family in Ireland* (Wicklow, 2004) p.167.
35 *Freeman's Journal*, 27 Sept. 1819; *Freeman's Journal*, 21 Aug. 1839.
36 Mount Jerome Historical project, *Mount Jerome – a Victorian cemetery* (Dublin, 1997) p. 5.

2. ACCUMULATORS, CONSOLIDATORS AND SPENDERS

1 Local Government Board, *Return of owners of land in Ireland* (Dublin, 1876) p. 20.
2 Shaw family papers, Family account book 1784–93 (NLI, MS 5610).
3 NLI, MS 5610.
4 http://safalra.com/other/historical-uk-inflation-price-conversion/ accessed 24th Sept. 2009.
5 NLI, MS 5610.
6 Shaw family papers, deeds and leases, 1707–1850 (NLI, MS 8939).
7 NLI, MS 5610.
8 NLI, MS 5610.
9 NLI, MS 5610.
10 NLI, MS 5610.
11 NLI, MS 5610.
12 NLI, MS 5610.
13 *Walker's Hibernian Magazine*, July 1796.
14 Shaw family papers, Letter book of Frederick Shaw 1846–59 (NLI, MS 5656).
15 http://www.twickenhamurc.org.uk /founder.htm, accessed 3 Aug. 2009.
16 *The Times*, 3 Feb. 1835.
17 *Freeman's Journal*, 2 Aug. 1821.
18 Shaw Collection (DCA, AR add/52/22).
19 *The Times*, 16 May 1837; *Freeman's Journal*, 21 Aug. 1839; 8 July 1819; 27 Dec. 1817; 3 Aug. 1835; 19 Feb. 1818; 9
    Sept. 1817; 13 Oct. 1817; 14 Nov. 1812; 18 Feb. 1796.
20 Lawrence James, *The middle class – a history* (London, 2006) p. 183.
21 *Pigot's directory*, 1824, p. 306.
22 Shaw family papers, Journal of Robert Shaw, second baronet (NLI, MS 3754).
23 NLI, MS 3754.
24 Last will and testament of Robert Shaw, second baronet (NAI, MS T8790).
25 NLI, MS 3754.
26 NLI, MS 3754.
27 NLI, MS 3754.
28 NLI, MS 3754.
29 NAI, Will of RS, second baronet, MS T8790.
30 Shaw family papers, Sundry deeds and papers, 1800–59 (NLI, MS D11, 545).
31 Shaw family papers, Domestic account books 1822–31 (NLI, MS 4711).
32 Last will and testament of Sir Robert Shaw, first baronet, 5th August 1839 (NAI, MS T8789).
33 NAI, Will of Robert Shaw, MS T8789.
34 NLI, MS 4711.
35 Shaw family papers, Terenure rent ledger 1869–76 (NLI, MS 9450).
36 *Irish Times & Daily Advertiser*, 12 Nov. 1869.
37 *Oxford dictionary of national biography* (Oxford, 2004), xvi, pp 81–2.
38 *Irish Times*, 25 Nov. 1834.
39 E. Moberly Bell, *Flora Shaw* (London, 1947), pp 12–13.
40 Ibid., p. 12.
41 The Sir Robert Peel collection, manuscript collection (BL, MS 40407 174).
42 NLI, MS 5656.
43 NLI, MS 5656.
44 NLI, MS 5656.
45 NLI, MS 5656.
46 NLI, MS 5656.
47 *Irish Times*, 7 July 1876.
48 *Freeman's Journal*, 24 Oct 1877.

3. POLITICIANS AND COMMUNITY ACTIVISTS

1 *First report of the commissioners appointed to inquire into municipal corporations in*

Ireland; Appendix (report on Dublin), H.C. 1835, xxvii, 154–5.

2 *Freeman's Journal,* 17 Oct. 1795.

3 E.M. Johnston-Liik, *History of the Irish parliament, 1692–1800* (6 vols Belfast, 2002), vi, p. 263.

4 Cullen papers (NLI, MS 9761, pp 34–6).

5 Johnston-Liik, *History of the Irish parliament,* vi, p. 263.

6 P.M. Geoghegan, 'The Irish house of commons, 1799–1800', in M. Brown, P.M. Geoghegan and J. Kelly (eds), *The Irish act of Union, 1800: bicentennial essays* (Dublin, 2003), p. 140.

7 Mc Ginley, *The La Touche family in Ireland,* p. 69.

8 B.M. Walker, *Parliamentary election results in Ireland, 1801–1922* (Dublin, 1978), p. 9.

9 M.E. Daly, *Dublin – the deposed capital: a social and economic history, 1860–1914* (Cork, 1984), p. 3.

10 *Freeman's Journal,* 17 Mar.1804

11 *Freeman's Journal,* 16 Oct. 1812.

12 *Freeman's Journal,* 27 Dec. 1809.

13 *Freeman's Journal,* 21 May 1810.

14 *Freeman's Journal,* 29 Oct. 1810.

15 *Freeman's Journal,* 17 Feb. 1817.

16 James Kelly, *Henry Grattan* (Dublin, 1993) p. 39.

17 Johnson-Liik, *History of the Irish parliament,* vi, p. 264.

18 *Freeman's Journal,* 3 Aug. 1813.

19 First report of the commissioners appointed to inquire into municipal corporations in Ireland; Appendix (report on Dublin) H.C. 1835, xxvii, 154–5.

20 *Burke's Peerage and Baronetage,* II, p. 2593.

21 V. Crossman, *Local government in nineteenth-century Ireland* (Belfast, 1994) p. 77.

22 *Calendar of the ancient records of Dublin* (Dublin, 1916), ed. Lady Gilbert, xvii p. 55.

23 Ibid., p. 137.

24 *Municipal Corporations enquiry,* H.C. 1835, xxvi, 154–5.

25 *Calendar of the ancient records,* xvii, pp 64–112.

26 *Calendar of the ancient records,* xvii, pp 136–7.

27 *Hansard 3,* xxix, 1312 (31 Jan. 1835).

28 Crossman, *Local government in nineteenth century,* p. 25.

29 Notes taken from the minutes of the County Dublin Grand Jury minute book for the years 1818/19, Fingal Council Archive, Swords, Co Dublin.

30 *The Times,* 14 Nov. 1827; 25 Nov. 1834.

31 C.L. Falkiner, *Sir Frederick Shaw, Oxford dictionary of national biography* (Oxford, 2004) [http://www.oxforddnb.com/view/article/25249, accessed 20 Sept. 2009]

32 *Oxford dictionary of national biography.*

33 P.V. Fitzpatrick, *Correspondence of Daniel O'Connell* (Dublin, 1888), I, pp 309–10.

34 Fitzpatrick, *Correspondence of O'Connell,* I, p. 32.

35 *Hansard 3,* lxxvii, 110 (4 Feb. 1845).

36 *Hansard 3,* lxxxiii, 731 (11 Feb. 1846).

37 *Hansard 3,* lxxxiii, 1075 (7 Feb. 1846).

38 *Hansard 3,* lxxxiii, 1075 (7 Feb. 1846).

39 RLFC papers (NAI, MS 3/2/9/36)

40 *Hansard 3,* lxxxiii, 1075 (7 Feb. 1846).

41 B. Walker, 'The Great Famine general election of 1847', *History Ireland,* 17:5 (Sept /Oct 2009), pp 27–30.

CONCLUSION

1. *Irish Times,* 3 Mar. 1953.